TITLE 4—FLAG AND SEAL, SEAT OF GOVERNMENT, AND THE STATES

This title was enacted by act July 30, 1947, ch. 389, § 1, 61 Stat. 641

AMENDMENTS

1951—Act Oct. 31, 1951, ch. 655, § 11, 65 Stat. 713, added item for chapter 5.

POSITIVE LAW; CITATION

This title has been made positive law by section 1 of act July 30, 1947, ch. 389, 61 Stat. 641, which provided in part that: "title 4 of the United States Code, entitled 'Flag and seal, Seat of Government, and the States', is codified and enacted into positive law and may be cited as '4 U. S. C., §—'".

REPEALS

Section 2 of act July 30, 1947, provided that the sections or parts thereof of the Statutes at Large or the Revised Statutes covering provisions codified in this Act are repealed insofar as the provisions appeared in former Title 4, and provided that any rights or liabilities now existing under the repealed sections or parts thereof shall not be affected by the repeal.

TABLE SHOWING DISPOSITION OF ALL SECTIONS OF FORMER TITLE 4

Title 4 Former Sections	Revised Statutes Statutes at Large	Title 4 New Sections
1	R.S. §§ 1791, 1792	1
2	R.S. § 1792	2
3	Feb. 8, 1917, ch. 34, 39 Stat. 900	3
4	R.S. § 1793	41
5	R.S. §§ 203 (first clause), 1794	42
6	R.S. § 1795	71
7	R.S. § 1796	72
8	R.S. § 4798	73
9	R.S. § 1836	101
10	R.S. § 1837	102
11	R.S. § 1838	103
12	June 16, 1936, ch. 582, § 10, 49 Stat. 1521	104
	Oct. 9, 1940, ch. 787, § 7, 54 Stat. 1060.	
13	Oct. 9, 1940, ch. 787, § 1, 54 Stat. 1059	105
14	Oct. 9, 1940, ch. 787, § 2, 54 Stat. 1060	106
15	Oct. 9, 1940, ch. 787, § 3, 54 Stat. 1060	107
16	Oct. 9, 1940, ch. 787, § 4, 54 Stat. 1060	108
17	Oct. 9, 1940, ch. 787, § 5, 54 Stat. 1060	109
18	Oct. 9, 1940, ch. 787, § 6, 54 Stat. 1060	110

CHAPTER 1—THE FLAG

AMENDMENTS

1998—Pub. L. 105–225, § 2(b), Aug. 12, 1998, 112 Stat. 1498, added items 4 to 10.

§ 1. Flag; stripes and stars on

The flag of the United States shall be thirteen horizontal stripes, alternate red and white; and the union of the flag shall be forty-eight stars, white in a blue field.

(July 30, 1947, ch. 389, 61 Stat. 642.)

SHORT TITLE OF 2009 AMENDMENT

Pub. L. 111–41, § 1, July 27, 2009, 123 Stat. 1962, provided that: "This Act [amending section 6 of this title] may be cited as the 'Korean War Veterans Recognition Act'."

SHORT TITLE OF 2007 AMENDMENT

Pub. L. 110–41, § 1, June 29, 2007, 121 Stat. 233, provided that: "This Act [amending section 7 of this title] may be cited as the 'Army Specialist Joseph P. Micks Federal Flag Code Amendment Act of 2007'."

SHORT TITLE OF 2000 AMENDMENT

Pub. L. 106–252, § 1, July 28, 2000, 114 Stat. 626, provided that: "This Act [enacting sections 116 to 126 of this title and provisions set out as a note under section 116 of this title] may be cited as the 'Mobile Telecommunications Sourcing Act'."

EXECUTIVE ORDER NO. 10798

Ex. Ord. No. 10798, Jan. 3, 1959, 24 F.R. 79, which prescribed proportions and sizes of flags until July 4, 1960, was revoked by section 33 of Ex. Ord. No. 10834, set out as a note under this section.

EX. ORD. NO. 10834. PROPORTIONS AND SIZES OF FLAGS AND POSITION OF STARS

Ex. Ord. No. 10834, Aug. 21, 1959, 24 F.R. 6865, provided:
WHEREAS the State of Hawaii has this day been admitted into the Union; and
WHEREAS section 2 of title 4 of the United States Code provides as follows: "On the admission of a new State into the Union one star shall be added to the union of the flag; and such addition shall take effect on the fourth day of July then next succeeding such admission."; and
WHEREAS the Federal Property and Administrative Services Act of 1949 (63 Stat. 377), as amended [see chapters 1 to 11 of Title 40, Public Buildings, Property, and Works, and division C (except sections 3302, 3307(e), 3501(b), 3509, 3906, 4710, and 4711) of subtitle I of Title 41, Public Contracts] authorizes the President to prescribe policies and directives governing the procurement and utilization of property by executive agencies; and

WHEREAS the interests of the Government require that orderly and reasonable provision be made for various matters pertaining to the flag and that appropriate regulations governing the procurement and utilization of national flags and union jacks by executive agencies be prescribed:

NOW, THEREFORE, by virtue of the authority vested in me as President of the United States and as Commander in Chief of the armed forces of the United States, and the Federal Property and Administrative Services Act of 1949, as amended [see Short Title of 1949 Act note under section 101 of Title 41, Public Contracts], it is hereby ordered as follows:

PART I—DESIGN OF THE FLAG

SECTION 1. The flag of the United States shall have thirteen horizontal stripes, alternate red and white, and a union consisting of white stars on a field of blue.

SEC. 2. The positions of the stars in the union of the flag and in the union jack shall be as indicated on the attachment to this order, which is hereby made a part of this order.

SEC. 3. The dimensions of the constituent parts of the flag shall conform to the proportions set forth in the attachment referred to in section 2 of this order.

PART II—REGULATIONS GOVERNING EXECUTIVE AGENCIES

SEC. 21. The following sizes of flags are authorized for executive agencies:

Size	Dimensions of Flag	
	Hoist (width)	Fly (length)
	Feet	Feet
(1)	20.00	38.00
(2)	10.00	19.00
(3)	8.95	17.00
(4)	7.00	11.00
(5)	5.00	9.50
(6)	4.33	5.50
(7)	3.50	6.65
(8)	3.00	4.00
(9)	3.00	5.70
(10)	2.37	4.50
(11)	1.32	2.50

SEC. 22. Flags manufactured or purchased for the use of executive agencies:

(a) Shall conform to the provisions of Part I of this order, except as may be otherwise authorized pursuant to the provisions of section 24, or except as otherwise authorized by the provisions of section 21, of this order.

(b) Shall conform to the provisions of section 21 of this order, except as may be otherwise authorized pursuant to the provisions of section 24 of this order.

SEC. 23. The exterior dimensions of each union jack manufactured or purchased for executive agencies shall equal the respective exterior dimensions of the union of a flag of a size authorized by or pursuant to this order. The size of the union jack flown with the national flag shall be the same as the size of the union of that national flag.

SEC. 24. (a) The Secretary of Defense in respect of procurement for the Department of Defense (including military colors) and the Administrator of General Services in respect of procurement for executive agencies other than the Department of Defense may, for cause which the Secretary or the Administrator, as the case may be, deems sufficient, make necessary minor adjustments in one or more of the dimensions or proportionate dimensions prescribed by this order, or authorize proportions or sizes other than those prescribed by section 3 or section 21 of this order.

(b) So far as practicable, (1) the actions of the Secretary of Defense under the provisions of section 24(a) of this order, as they relate to the various organizational elements of the Department of Defense, shall be coordinated, and (2) the Secretary and the Administrator shall mutually coordinate their actions under that section.

SEC. 25. Subject to such limited exceptions as the Secretary of Defense in respect of the Department of Defense, and the Administrator of General Services in respect of executive agencies other than the Department of Defense, may approve, all national flags and union jacks now in the possession of executive agencies, or hereafter acquired by executive agencies under contracts awarded prior to the date of this order, including those so possessed or so acquired by the General Services Administration, for distribution to other agencies, shall be utilized until unserviceable.

PART III—GENERAL PROVISIONS

SEC. 31. The flag prescribed by Executive Order No. 10798 of January 3, 1959, shall be the official flag of the United States until July 4, 1960, and on that date the flag prescribed by Part I of this order shall become the official flag of the United States; but this section shall neither derogate from section 24 or section 25 of this order nor preclude the procurement, for executive agencies, of flags provided for by or pursuant to this order at any time after the date of this order.

SEC. 32. As used in this order, the term "executive agencies" means the executive departments and independent establishments in the executive branch of the Government, including wholly-owned Government corporations.

SEC. 33. Executive Order No. 10798 of January 3, 1959, is hereby revoked.

DWIGHT D. EISENHOWER.

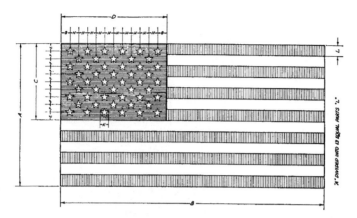

Standard proportions

Hoist (width) of flag 1.0	Fly (length) of flag 1.9	Hoist (width) of Union 0.5385 (7/13)	Fly (length) of Union 0.76	0.054	0.054	0.063	0.063	Diameter of star 0.0616	Width of stripe 0.0769 (1/13)
A	B	C	D	E	F	G	H	K	L

§ 2. Same; additional stars

On the admission of a new State into the Union one star shall be added to the union of the flag; and such addition shall take effect on the fourth day of July then next succeeding such admission.

(July 30, 1947, ch. 389, 61 Stat. 642.)

§ 3. Use of flag for advertising purposes; mutilation of flag

Any person who, within the District of Columbia, in any manner, for exhibition or display, shall place or cause to be placed any word, figure, mark, picture, design, drawing, or any advertisement of any nature upon any flag, standard, colors, or ensign of the United States of America; or shall expose or cause to be exposed to public view any such flag, standard, colors, or ensign upon which shall have been printed, painted, or otherwise placed, or to which shall be attached, appended, affixed, or annexed any word, figure, mark, picture, design, or drawing, or any advertisement of any nature; or who, within the District of Columbia, shall manufacture, sell, expose for sale, or to public view, or give away or have in possession for sale, or to be given away or for use for any purpose, any article or substance being an article of merchandise, or a receptacle for merchandise or article or thing for carrying or transporting merchandise, upon which shall have been printed, painted, attached, or otherwise placed a representation of any such flag, standard, colors, or ensign, to advertise, call attention to, decorate, mark, or distinguish the article or substance on which so placed shall be deemed guilty of a misdemeanor and shall be punished by a fine not exceeding

$100 or by imprisonment for not more than thirty days, or both, in the discretion of the court. The words "flag, standard, colors, or ensign", as used herein, shall include any flag, standard, colors, ensign, or any picture or representation of either, or of any part or parts of either, made of any substance or represented on any substance, of any size evidently purporting to be either of said flag, standard, colors, or ensign of the United States of America or a picture or a representation of either, upon which shall be shown the colors, the stars and the stripes, in any number of either thereof, or of any part or parts of either, by which the average person seeing the same without deliberation may believe the same to represent the flag, colors, standard, or ensign of the United States of America.

(July 30, 1947, ch. 389, 61 Stat. 642; Pub. L. 90–381, § 3, July 5, 1968, 82 Stat. 291.)

AMENDMENTS

1968—Pub. L. 90–381 struck out "; or who, within the District of Columbia, shall publicly mutilate, deface, defile or defy, trample upon, or cast contempt, either by word or act, upon any such flag, standard, colors, or ensign," after "substance on which so placed".

§ 4. Pledge of allegiance to the flag; manner of delivery

The Pledge of Allegiance to the Flag: "I pledge allegiance to the Flag of the United States of America, and to the Republic for which it stands, one Nation under God, indivisible, with liberty and justice for all.", should be rendered by standing at attention facing the flag with the right hand over the heart. When not in uniform men should remove any non-religious headdress with their right hand and hold it at the left shoulder, the hand being over the heart. Persons in uniform should remain silent, face the flag, and render the military salute.

(Added Pub. L. 105–225, § 2(a), Aug. 12, 1998, 112 Stat. 1494; amended Pub. L. 107–293, § 2(a), Nov. 13, 2002, 116 Stat. 2060.)

HISTORICAL AND REVISION NOTES

Revised Section	Source (U.S. Code)	Source (Statutes at Large)
4	36:172.	June 22, 1942, ch. 435, § 7, 56 Stat. 380; Dec. 22, 1942, ch. 806, § 7, 56 Stat. 1077; Dec. 28, 1945, ch. 607, 59 Stat. 668; June 14, 1954, ch. 297, 68 Stat. 249; July 7, 1976, Pub. L. 94–344, (19), 90 Stat. 813.

CODIFICATION

Amendment by Pub. L. 107–293 reaffirmed the exact language of the Pledge, see section 2(b) of Pub. L. 107–293, set out as a Reaffirmation of Language note below.

AMENDMENTS

2002—Pub. L. 107–293 reenacted section catchline without change and amended text generally. Prior to amendment, text read as follows: "The Pledge of Allegiance to the Flag, 'I pledge allegiance to the Flag of the United States of America, and to the Republic for which it stands, one Nation under God, indivisible, with liberty and justice for all.', should be rendered by standing at attention facing the flag with the right hand over the heart. When not in uniform men should remove their headdress with their right hand and hold it at the left shoulder, the hand being over the heart. Persons in uniform should remain silent, face the flag, and render the military salute."

FINDINGS

Pub. L. 107–293, § 1, Nov. 13, 2002, 116 Stat. 2057, provided that: "Congress finds the following:

"(1) On November 11, 1620, prior to embarking for the shores of America, the Pilgrims signed the Mayflower Compact that declared: 'Having undertaken, for the Glory of God and the advancement of the Christian Faith and honor of our King and country, a voyage to plant the first colony in the northern parts of Virginia,'.

"(2) On July 4, 1776, America's Founding Fathers, after appealing to the 'Laws of Nature, and of Nature's God' to justify their separation from Great Britain, then declared: 'We hold these Truths to be self-evident, that all Men are created equal, that they are endowed by their Creator with certain unalienable Rights, that among these are Life, Liberty, and the Pursuit of Happiness'.

"(3) In 1781, Thomas Jefferson, the author of the Declaration of Independence and later the Nation's third President, in his work titled 'Notes on the State of Virginia' wrote: 'God who gave us life gave us liberty. And can the liberties of a nation be thought secure when we have removed their only firm basis, a conviction in the minds of the people that these liberties are of the Gift of God. That they are not to be violated but with His wrath? Indeed, I tremble for my country when I reflect that God is just; that his justice cannot sleep forever.'

"(4) On May 14, 1787, George Washington, as President of the Constitutional Convention, rose to admonish and exhort the delegates and declared: 'If to please the people we offer what we ourselves disapprove, how can we afterward defend our work? Let us raise a standard to which the wise and the honest can repair; the event is in the hand of God!'

"(5) On July 21, 1789, on the same day that it approved the Establishment Clause concerning religion,

the First Congress of the United States also passed the Northwest Ordinance, providing for a territorial government for lands northwest of the Ohio River, which declared: 'Religion, morality, and knowledge, being necessary to good government and the happiness of mankind, schools and the means of education shall forever be encouraged.'

"(6) On September 25, 1789, the First Congress unanimously approved a resolution calling on President George Washington to proclaim a National Day of Thanksgiving for the people of the United States by declaring, 'a day of public thanksgiving and prayer, to be observed by acknowledging, with grateful hearts, the many signal favors of Almighty God, especially by affording them an opportunity peaceably to establish a constitution of government for their safety and happiness.'

"(7) On November 19, 1863, President Abraham Lincoln delivered his Gettysburg Address on the site of the battle and declared: 'It is rather for us to be here dedicated to the great task remaining before us—that from these honored dead we take increased devotion to that cause for which they gave the last full measure of devotion—that we here highly resolve that these dead shall not have died in vain—that this Nation, under God, shall have a new birth of freedom—and that Government of the people, by the people, for the people, shall not perish from the earth.'

"(8) On April 28, 1952, in the decision of the Supreme Court of the United States in Zorach v. Clauson, 343 U.S. 306 (1952), in which school children were allowed to be excused from public schools for religious observances and education, Justice William O. Douglas, in writing for the Court stated: 'The First Amendment, however, does not say that in every and all respects there shall be a separation of Church and State. Rather, it studiously defines the manner, the specific ways, in which there shall be no concern or union or dependency one on the other. That is the common sense of the matter. Otherwise the State and religion would be aliens to each other—hostile, suspicious, and even unfriendly. Churches could not be required to pay even property taxes. Municipalities would not be permitted to render police or fire protection to religious groups. Policemen who helped parishioners into their places of worship would violate the Constitution. Prayers in our legislative halls; the appeals to the Almighty in the messages of the Chief Executive; the proclamations making Thanksgiving Day a holiday; "so help me God" in our courtroom oaths—these and all other references to the Almighty that run through our laws, our public rituals, our ceremonies would be flouting the First Amendment. A fastidious atheist or agnostic could even object to the supplication with which the Court opens each session: "God save the United States and this Honorable Court."'

"(9) On June 15, 1954, Congress passed and President Eisenhower signed into law a statute that was clearly consistent with the text and intent of the Constitution of the United States, that amended the Pledge of Allegiance to read: 'I pledge allegiance to the Flag of the United States of America and to the Republic for which it stands, one Nation under God, indivisible, with liberty and justice for all.'

"(10) On July 20, 1956, Congress proclaimed that the national motto of the United States is 'In God We Trust', and that motto is inscribed above the main door of the Senate, behind the Chair of the Speaker of the House of Representatives, and on the currency of the United States.

"(11) On June 17, 1963, in the decision of the Supreme Court of the United States in Abington School District v. Schempp, 374 U.S. 203 (1963), in which compulsory school prayer was held unconstitutional, Justices Goldberg and Harlan, concurring in the decision, stated: 'But untutored devotion to the concept of neutrality can lead to invocation or approval of results which partake not simply of that noninterference and noninvolvement with the religious which the Constitution commands, but of a brooding and pervasive devotion to the secular and a passive, or even active, hostility to the religious. Such results are not only not compelled by the Constitution, but, it seems to me, are prohibited by it. Neither government nor this Court can or should ignore the significance of the fact that a vast portion of our people believe in and worship God and that many of our legal, political, and personal values derive historically from religious teachings. Government must inevitably take cognizance of the existence of religion and, indeed, under certain circumstances the First Amendment may require that it do so.'

"(12) On March 5, 1984, in the decision of the Supreme Court of the United States in Lynch v. Donelly, 465 U.S. 668 (1984), in which a city government's display of a nativity scene was held to be constitutional, Chief Justice Burger, writing for the Court, stated: 'There is an unbroken history of official acknowledgment by all three branches of government of the role of religion in American life from at least 1789 . . . [E]xamples of reference to our religious heritage are found in the statutorily prescribed national motto "In God We Trust" (36 U.S.C. 186) [now 36 U.S.C. 302], which Congress and the President mandated for our currency, see (31 U.S.C. 5112(d)(1) (1982 ed.)), and in the language "One Nation under God", as part of the Pledge of Allegiance to the American flag. That pledge is recited by many thousands of public school children—and adults—every year . . . Art galleries supported by public revenues display religious paintings of the 15th and 16th centuries, predominantly inspired by one religious faith. The National Gallery in Washington, maintained with Government support, for example, has long exhibited masterpieces with religious messages, notably the Last Supper, and paintings depicting the Birth of Christ, the Crucifixion, and the Resurrection, among many others with explicit Christian themes and messages. The very chamber in which oral arguments on this case were heard is decorated with a notable and permanent—not seasonal—symbol of religion: Moses with the Ten Commandments. Congress has long provided chapels in the Capitol for religious worship and meditation.'

"(13) On June 4, 1985, in the decision of the Supreme Court of the United States in Wallace v. Jaffree, 472 U.S. 38 (1985), in which a mandatory moment of silence to be used for meditation or voluntary prayer was held unconstitutional, Justice O'Connor, concurring in the judgment and addressing the contention that the Court's holding would render the Pledge of Allegiance unconstitutional because Congress amended it in 1954 to add the words 'under God,' stated 'In my view, the words "under God" in the Pledge, as codified at (36 U.S.C. 172) [now 4 U.S.C. 4], serve as an acknowledgment of religion with "the legitimate secular purposes of solemnizing public occasions, [and] expressing confidence in the future."'

"(14) On November 20, 1992, the United States Court of Appeals for the 7th Circuit, in Sherman v. Community Consolidated School District 21, 980 F.2d 437 (7th Cir. 1992), held that a school district's policy for voluntary recitation of the Pledge of Allegiance including the words 'under God' was constitutional.

"(15) The 9th Circuit Court of Appeals erroneously held, in Newdow v. U.S. Congress (9th Cir. June 26, 2002), that the Pledge of Allegiance's use of the express religious reference 'under God' violates the First Amendment to the Constitution, and that, therefore, a school district's policy and practice of teacher-led voluntary recitations of the Pledge of Allegiance is unconstitutional.

"(16) The erroneous rationale of the 9th Circuit Court of Appeals in Newdow would lead to the absurd result that the Constitution's use of the express religious reference 'Year of our Lord' in Article VII violates the First Amendment to the Constitution, and that, therefore, a school district's policy and practice of teacher-led voluntary recitations of the Constitution itself would be unconstitutional."

REAFFIRMATION OF LANGUAGE

Pub. L. 107–293, §2(b), Nov. 13, 2002, 116 Stat. 2060, provided that: "In codifying this subsection [probably should be "section", meaning section 2 of Pub. L. 107–293, which amended this section], the Office of the Law Revision Counsel shall show in the historical and statutory notes that the 107th Congress reaffirmed the exact language that has appeared in the Pledge for decades."

§ 5. Display and use of flag by civilians; codification of rules and customs; definition

The following codification of existing rules and customs pertaining to the display and use of the flag of the United States of America is established for the use of such civilians or civilian groups or organizations as may not be required to conform with regulations promulgated by one or more executive departments of the Government of the United States. The flag of the United States for the purpose of this chapter shall be defined according to sections 1 and 2 of this title and Executive Order 10834 issued pursuant thereto.

(Added Pub. L. 105–225, §2(a), Aug. 12, 1998, 112 Stat. 1494.)

HISTORICAL AND REVISION NOTES

Revised Section	Source (U.S. Code)	Source (Statutes at Large)
5	36:173.	June 22, 1942, ch. 435, §1, 56 Stat. 377; Dec. 22, 1942, ch. 806, §1, 56 Stat. 1074; July 7, 1976, Pub. L. 94–344, (1), 90 Stat. 810.

REFERENCES IN TEXT

Executive Order 10834, referred to in text, is set out as a note under section 1 of this title.

FREEDOM TO DISPLAY THE AMERICAN FLAG

Pub. L. 109–243, July 24, 2006, 120 Stat. 572, provided that:

"SECTION 1. SHORT TITLE.

"This Act may be cited as the 'Freedom to Display the American Flag Act of 2005'.

"SEC. 2. DEFINITIONS.

"For purposes of this Act—
  "(1) the term 'flag of the United States' has the meaning given the term 'flag, standard, colors, or ensign' under section 3 of title 4, United States Code;
  "(2) the terms 'condominium association' and 'cooperative association' have the meanings given such terms under section 604 of Public Law 96–399 (15 U.S.C. 3603);
  "(3) the term 'residential real estate management association' has the meaning given such term under section 528 of the Internal Revenue Code of 1986 (26 U.S.C. 528); and
  "(4) the term 'member'—
    "(A) as used with respect to a condominium association, means an owner of a condominium unit (as defined under section 604 of Public Law 96–399 (15 U.S.C. 3603)) within such association;
    "(B) as used with respect to a cooperative association, means a cooperative unit owner (as defined under section 604 of Public Law 96–399 (15 U.S.C. 3603)) within such association; and
    "(C) as used with respect to a residential real estate management association, means an owner of a residential property within a subdivision, development, or similar area subject to any policy or restriction adopted by such association.

"SEC. 3. RIGHT TO DISPLAY THE FLAG OF THE UNITED STATES.

"A condominium association, cooperative association, or residential real estate management association may not adopt or enforce any policy, or enter into any agreement, that would restrict or prevent a member of the association from displaying the flag of the United States on residential property within the association with respect to which such member has a separate ownership interest or a right to exclusive possession or use.

"SEC. 4. LIMITATIONS.

"Nothing in this Act shall be considered to permit any display or use that is inconsistent with—

"(1) any provision of chapter 1 of title 4, United States Code, or any rule or custom pertaining to the proper display or use of the flag of the United States (as established pursuant to such chapter or any otherwise applicable provision of law); or

"(2) any reasonable restriction pertaining to the time, place, or manner of displaying the flag of the United States necessary to protect a substantial interest of the condominium association, cooperative association, or residential real estate management association."

§ 6. Time and occasions for display

(a) It is the universal custom to display the flag only from sunrise to sunset on buildings and on stationary flagstaffs in the open. However, when a patriotic effect is desired, the flag may be displayed 24 hours a day if properly illuminated during the hours of darkness.

(b) The flag should be hoisted briskly and lowered ceremoniously.

(c) The flag should not be displayed on days when the weather is inclement, except when an all weather flag is displayed.

(d) The flag should be displayed on all days, especially on New Year's Day, January 1; Inauguration Day, January 20; Martin Luther King Jr.'s birthday, third Monday in January; Lincoln's Birthday, February 12; Washington's Birthday, third Monday in February; Easter Sunday (variable); Mother's Day, second Sunday in May; Armed Forces Day, third Saturday in May; Memorial Day (half-staff until noon), the last Monday in May; Flag Day, June 14; Father's Day, third Sunday in June; Independence Day, July 4; National Korean War Veterans Armistice Day, July 27; Labor Day, first Monday in September; Constitution Day, September 17; Columbus Day, second Monday in October; Navy Day, October 27; Veterans Day, November 11; Thanksgiving Day, fourth Thursday in November; Christmas Day, December 25; and such other days as may be proclaimed by the President of the United States; the birthdays of States (date of admission); and on State holidays.

(e) The flag should be displayed daily on or near the main administration building of every public institution.

(f) The flag should be displayed in or near every polling place on election days.

(g) The flag should be displayed during school days in or near every schoolhouse.

(Added Pub. L. 105–225, § 2(a), Aug. 12, 1998, 112 Stat. 1494; amended Pub. L. 106–80, § 1, Oct. 25, 1999, 113 Stat. 1285; Pub. L. 110–239, § 1, June 3, 2008, 122 Stat. 1559; Pub. L. 111–41, § 2, July 27, 2009, 123 Stat. 1962.)

HISTORICAL AND REVISION NOTES

Revised Section	Source (U.S. Code)	Source (Statutes at Large)
6	36:174.	June 22, 1942, ch. 435, § 2, 56 Stat. 378; Dec. 22, 1942, ch. 806, § 2, 56 Stat. 1074; July 7, 1976, Pub. L. 94–344, (2)–(5), 90 Stat. 810.

In subsection (d), the words "Veterans Day" are substituted for "Armistice Day" because of the Act of June 1, 1954 (ch. 250, 68 Stat. 168).

AMENDMENTS

2009—Subsec. (d). Pub. L. 111–41 inserted "National Korean War Veterans Armistice Day, July 27;" after "July 4;".
2008—Subsec. (d). Pub. L. 110–239 inserted "Father's Day, third Sunday in June;" after "Flag Day, June 14;".
1999—Subsec. (d). Pub. L. 106–80 inserted "Martin Luther King Jr.'s birthday, third Monday in January;" after "January 20;".

§ 7. Position and manner of display

The flag, when carried in a procession with another flag or flags, should be either on the marching right; that is, the flag's own right, or, if there is a line of other flags, in front of the center of that line.

(a) The flag should not be displayed on a float in a parade except from a staff, or as provided in subsection (i) of this section.

(b) The flag should not be draped over the hood, top, sides, or back of a vehicle or of a railroad train or a boat. When the flag is displayed on a motorcar, the staff shall be fixed firmly to the chassis or clamped to the right fender.

(c) No other flag or pennant should be placed above or, if on the same level, to the right of the flag of the United States of America, except during church services conducted by naval chaplains at sea, when the church pennant may be flown above the flag during church services for the personnel of the Navy. No person shall display the flag of the United Nations or any other national or international flag equal, above, or in a position of superior prominence or honor to, or in place of, the flag of the United States at any place within the United States or any Territory or possession thereof: Provided, That nothing in this section shall make unlawful the continuance of the practice heretofore followed of displaying the flag of the United Nations in a position of superior prominence or honor, and other national flags in positions of equal prominence or honor, with that of the flag of the United States at the headquarters of the United Nations.

(d) The flag of the United States of America, when it is displayed with another flag against a wall from crossed staffs, should be on the right, the flag's own right, and its staff should be in front of the staff of the other flag.

(e) The flag of the United States of America should be at the center and at the highest point of the group when a number of flags of States or localities or pennants of societies are grouped and displayed from staffs.

(f) When flags of States, cities, or localities, or pennants of societies are flown on the same halyard with the flag of the United States, the latter should always be at the peak. When the flags are flown from adjacent staffs, the flag of the United States should be hoisted first and lowered last. No such flag or pennant may be placed above the flag of the United States or to the United States flag's right.

(g) When flags of two or more nations are displayed, they are to be flown from separate staffs of the same height. The flags should be of approximately equal size. International usage forbids the display of the flag of one nation above that of another nation in time of peace.

(h) When the flag of the United States is displayed from a staff projecting horizontally or at an angle from the window sill, balcony, or front of a building, the union of the flag should be placed at the peak of the staff unless the flag is at half-staff. When the flag is suspended over a sidewalk from a rope extending from a house to a pole at the edge of the sidewalk, the flag should be hoisted out, union first, from the building.

(i) When displayed either horizontally or vertically against a wall, the union should be uppermost and to the flag's own right, that is, to the observer's left. When displayed in a window, the flag should be displayed in the same way, with the union or blue field to the left of the observer in the street.

(j) When the flag is displayed over the middle of the street, it should be suspended vertically with the union to the north in an east and west street or to the east in a north and south street.

(k) When used on a speaker's platform, the flag, if displayed flat, should be displayed above and behind the speaker. When displayed from a staff in a church or public auditorium, the flag of the United States of America should hold the position of superior prominence, in advance of the audience, and in the position of honor at the clergyman's or speaker's right as he faces the audience. Any other flag so displayed should be placed on the left of the clergyman or speaker or to the right of the audience.

(l) The flag should form a distinctive feature of the ceremony of unveiling a statue or monument, but it should never be used as the covering for the statue or monument.

(m) The flag, when flown at half-staff, should be first hoisted to the peak for an instant and then lowered to the half-staff position. The flag should be again raised to the peak before it is lowered for the day. On Memorial Day the flag should be displayed at half-staff until noon only, then raised to the top of the staff. By order of the President, the flag shall be flown at half-staff upon the death of principal figures of the United States Government and the Governor of a State, territory, or possession, as a mark of respect to their memory. In the event of the death of other officials or foreign dignitaries, the flag is to be displayed at half-staff according to Presidential instructions or orders, or in accordance with recognized customs or practices not inconsistent with law. In the event of the death of a present or former official of the government of any State, territory, or possession of the United States or the death of a member of the Armed Forces from any State, territory, or possession who dies while serving on active duty, the Governor of that State, territory, or possession may proclaim that the National flag shall be flown at half-staff, and the same authority is provided to the Mayor of the District of Columbia with respect to present or former officials of the District of Columbia and members of the Armed Forces from the District of Columbia. When the Governor of a State, territory, or possession, or the Mayor of the District of Columbia, issues a proclamation under the preceding sentence that the National flag be flown at half-staff in that State, territory, or possession or in the District of Columbia because of the death of a member of the Armed Forces, the National flag flown at any Federal installation or facility in the area covered by that proclamation shall be flown at half-staff consistent with that proclamation. The flag shall be flown at half-staff 30 days from the death of the President or a former President; 10 days from the day of death of the Vice President, the Chief Justice or a retired Chief Justice of the United States, or the Speaker of the House of Representatives; from the day of death until interment of an Associate Justice of the Supreme Court, a Secretary of an executive or military department, a former Vice President, or the Governor of a State, territory, or possession; and on the day of death and the following day for a Member of Congress. The flag shall be flown at half-staff on Peace Officers Memorial Day, unless that day is also Armed Forces Day. As used in this subsection—

(1) the term "half-staff" means the position of the flag when it is one-half the distance between the top and bottom of the staff;

(2) the term "executive or military department" means any agency listed under sections 101 and 102 of title 5, United States Code; and

(3) the term "Member of Congress" means a Senator, a Representative, a Delegate, or the Resident Commissioner from Puerto Rico.

(n) When the flag is used to cover a casket, it should be so placed that the union is at the head and over the left shoulder. The flag should not be lowered into the grave or allowed to touch the ground.

(o) When the flag is suspended across a corridor or lobby in a building with only one main entrance, it should be suspended vertically with the union of the flag to the observer's left upon entering. If the building has more than one main entrance, the flag should be suspended vertically near the center of the corridor or lobby with the union to the north, when entrances are to the east and west or to the east when entrances are to the north and south. If there are entrances in more than two directions, the union should be to the east.

(Added Pub. L. 105–225, § 2(a), Aug. 12, 1998, 112 Stat. 1495; amended Pub. L. 110–41, § 3, June 29, 2007, 121 Stat. 233.)

HISTORICAL AND REVISION NOTES

Revised Section	Source (U.S. Code)	Source (Statutes at Large)
7	36:175.	June 22, 1942, ch. 435, § 3, 56 Stat. 378; Dec. 22, 1942, ch. 806, § 3, 56 Stat. 1075; July 9, 1953, ch. 183, 67 Stat. 142; July 7, 1976, Pub. L. 94–344, (6)–(11), 90 Stat. 811; Sept. 13, 1994, Pub. L. 103–322, title XXXII, § 320922(b), 108 Stat. 2131.

AMENDMENTS

2007—Subsec. (m). Pub. L. 110–41, in sixth sentence, inserted "or the death of a member of the Armed Forces from any State, territory, or possession who dies while serving on active duty" after "present or former official of the government of any State, territory, or possession of the United States" and substituted ", and the same authority is provided to the Mayor of the District of Columbia with respect to present or former officials of the District of Columbia and members of the Armed Forces from the District of Columbia. When the Governor of a State, territory, or possession, or the Mayor of the District of Columbia, issues a proclamation under the preceding sentence that the National flag be flown at half-staff in that State, territory, or possession or in the District of Columbia because of the death of a member of the Armed Forces, the National flag flown at any Federal installation or facility in the area covered by that proclamation shall be flown at half-staff consistent with that proclamation." for period at end.

FINDING

Pub. L. 110–41, § 2, June 29, 2007, 121 Stat. 233, provided that: "Congress finds that members of the Armed Forces of the United States defend the freedom and security of the United States."

PROC. NO. 3044. DISPLAY OF FLAG AT HALF-STAFF UPON DEATH OF CERTAIN OFFICIALS AND FORMER OFFICIALS

Proc. No. 3044, Mar. 1, 1954, 19 F.R. 1235, as amended by Proc. No. 3948, Dec. 12, 1969, 34 F.R. 19699, provided:

WHEREAS it is appropriate that the flag of the United States of America be flown at half-staff on Federal buildings, grounds, and facilities upon the death of principal officials and former officials of the Government of the United States and the Governors of the States, Territories, and possessions of the United States as a mark of respect to their memory; and

WHEREAS it is desirable that rules be prescribed for the uniform observance of this mark of respect by all executive departments and agencies of the Government, and as a guide to the people of the Nation generally on such occasions:

NOW, THEREFORE, I, DWIGHT D. EISENHOWER, President of the United States of America and Commander in Chief of the armed forces of the United States, do hereby prescribe and proclaim the following rules with respect to the display of the flag of the United States of America at half-staff upon the death of the officials hereinafter designated:

1. The flag of the United States shall be flown at half-staff on all buildings, grounds, and naval vessels of the Federal Government in the District of Columbia and throughout the United States and its Territories and possessions for the period indicated upon the death of any of the following-designated officials or former officials of the United States:

(a) The President or a former President: for thirty days from the day of death.

The flag shall also be flown at half-staff for such period at all United States embassies, legations, and other facilities abroad, including all military facilities and naval vessels and stations.

(b) The Vice President, the Chief Justice or a retired Chief Justice of the United States, or the Speaker of the House of Representatives: for ten days from the day of death.

(c) An Associate Justice of the Supreme Court, a member of the Cabinet, a former Vice President, the President pro tempore of the Senate, the Majority Leader of the Senate, the Minority Leader of the Senate, the Majority Leader of the House of Representatives, or the Minority Leader of the House of Representatives: from the day of death until interment.

2. The flag of the United States shall be flown at half-staff on all buildings, grounds, and naval vessels of the Federal Government in the metropolitan area of the District of Columbia on the day of death and on the following day upon the death of a United States Senator, Representative, Territorial Delegate, or the Resident Commissioner from the Commonwealth of Puerto Rico, and it shall also be flown at half-staff on all buildings, grounds, and naval vessels of the Federal Government in the State, Congressional District, Territory, or Commonwealth of such Senator, Representative, Delegate, or Commissioner, respectively, from the day of death until interment.

3. The flag of the United States shall be flown at half-staff on all buildings and grounds of the Federal Government in a State, Territory, or possession of the United States upon the death of the Governor of such State, Territory, or possession from the day of death until interment.

4. In the event of the death of other officials, former officials, or foreign dignitaries, the flag of the United States shall be displayed at half-staff in accordance with such orders or instructions as may be issued by or at the direction of the President, or in accordance with recognized customs or practices not inconsistent with law.

5. The heads of the several departments and agencies of the Government may direct that the flag of the United States be flown at half-staff on buildings, grounds, or naval vessels under their jurisdiction on occasions other than those specified herein which they consider proper, and that suitable military honors be rendered as appropriate.

IN WITNESS WHEREOF, I have hereunto set my hand and caused the Seal of the United States of America to be affixed.

DONE at the City of Washington this 1st day of March in the year of our Lord nineteen hundred and fifty-four, and of the Independence of the United States of America the one hundred and seventy-eighth.

[SEAL]

DWIGHT D. EISENHOWER.

§ 8. Respect for flag

No disrespect should be shown to the flag of the United States of America; the flag should not be dipped to any person or thing. Regimental colors, State flags, and organization or institutional flags are to be dipped as a mark of honor.

(a) The flag should never be displayed with the union down, except as a signal of dire distress in instances of extreme danger to life or property.

(b) The flag should never touch anything beneath it, such as the ground, the floor, water, or merchandise.

(c) The flag should never be carried flat or horizontally, but always aloft and free.

(d) The flag should never be used as wearing apparel, bedding, or drapery. It should never be festooned, drawn back, nor up, in folds, but always allowed to fall free. Bunting of blue, white, and red, always arranged with the blue above, the white in the middle, and the red below, should be used for covering a speaker's desk, draping the front of the platform, and for decoration in general.

(e) The flag should never be fastened, displayed, used, or stored in such a manner as to permit it to be easily torn, soiled, or damaged in any way.

(f) The flag should never be used as a covering for a ceiling.

(g) The flag should never have placed upon it, nor on any part of it, nor attached to it any mark, insignia, letter, word, figure, design, picture, or drawing of any nature.

(h) The flag should never be used as a receptacle for receiving, holding, carrying, or delivering anything.

(i) The flag should never be used for advertising purposes in any manner whatsoever. It should not be embroidered on such articles as cushions or handkerchiefs and the like, printed or otherwise impressed on paper napkins or boxes or anything that is designed for temporary use and discard. Advertising signs should not be fastened to a staff or halyard from which the flag is flown.

(j) No part of the flag should ever be used as a costume or athletic uniform. However, a flag patch may be affixed to the uniform of military personnel, firemen, policemen, and members of patriotic organizations. The flag represents a living country and is itself considered a living thing. Therefore, the lapel flag pin being a replica, should be worn on the left lapel near the heart.

(k) The flag, when it is in such condition that it is no longer a fitting emblem for display, should be destroyed in a dignified way, preferably by burning.

(Added Pub. L. 105–225, §2(a), Aug. 12, 1998, 112 Stat. 1497.)

HISTORICAL AND REVISION NOTES

Revised Section	Source (U.S. Code)	Source (Statutes at Large)
8	36:176.	June 22, 1942, ch. 435, §4, 56 Stat. 379; Dec. 22, 1942, ch. 806, §4, 56 Stat. 1076; July 7, 1976, Pub. L. 94–344, (12)–(16), 90 Stat. 812.

§ 9. Conduct during hoisting, lowering or passing of flag

During the ceremony of hoisting or lowering the flag or when the flag is passing in a parade or in review, all persons present in uniform should render the military salute. Members of the Armed Forces and veterans who are present but not in uniform may render the military salute. All other persons present should face the flag and stand at attention with their right hand over the heart, or if applicable, remove their headdress with their right hand and hold it at the left shoulder, the hand being over the heart. Citizens of other countries present should stand at attention. All such conduct toward the flag in a moving column should be rendered at the moment the flag passes.

(Added Pub. L. 105–225, §2(a), Aug. 12, 1998, 112 Stat. 1498; Pub. L. 110–181, div. A, title V, §594, Jan. 28, 2008, 122 Stat. 138.)

HISTORICAL AND REVISION NOTES

Revised Section	Source (U.S. Code)	Source (Statutes at Large)
9	36:177.	June 22, 1942, ch. 435, §5, 56 Stat. 380; Dec. 22, 1942, ch. 806, §5, 56 Stat. 1077; July 7, 1976, Pub. L. 94–344, (17), 90 Stat. 812.

AMENDMENTS

2008—Pub. L. 110–181 substituted "all persons present in uniform should render the military salute. Members of the Armed Forces and veterans who are present but not in uniform may render the military salute. All other persons present should face the flag and stand at attention with their right hand over the heart, or if applicable, remove their headdress with their right hand

and hold it at the left shoulder, the hand being over the heart. Citizens of other countries present should stand at attention. All such conduct toward the flag in a moving column should be rendered at the moment the flag passes." for "all persons present except those in uniform should face the flag and stand at attention with the right hand over the heart. Those present in uniform should render the military salute. When not in uniform, men should remove their headdress with their right hand and hold it at the left shoulder, the hand being over the heart. Aliens should stand at attention. The salute to the flag in a moving column should be rendered at the moment the flag passes."

§ 10. Modification of rules and customs by President

Any rule or custom pertaining to the display of the flag of the United States of America, set forth herein, may be altered, modified, or repealed, or additional rules with respect thereto may be prescribed, by the Commander in Chief of the Armed Forces of the United States, whenever he deems it to be appropriate or desirable; and any such alteration or additional rule shall be set forth in a proclamation.

(Added Pub. L. 105–225, §2(a), Aug. 12, 1998, 112 Stat. 1498.)

HISTORICAL AND REVISION NOTES

Revised Section	Source (U.S. Code)	Source (Statutes at Large)
10	36:178.	June 22, 1942, ch. 435, §8, 56 Stat. 380; Dec. 22, 1942, ch. 806, §8, 56 Stat. 1077; July 7, 1976, Pub. L. 94–344, (20), 90 Stat. 813.

REFERENCES IN TEXT

Herein, referred to in text, means sections 4 to 10 of this title.

PROC. NO. 2605. THE FLAG OF THE UNITED STATES

Proc. No. 2605, Feb. 18, 1944, 9 F.R. 1957, 58 Stat. 1126, provided:

The flag of the United States of America is universally representative of the principles of the justice, liberty, and democracy enjoyed by the people of the United States; and

People all over the world recognize the flag of the United States as symbolic of the United States; and

The effective prosecution of the war requires a proper understanding by the people of other countries of the material assistance being given by the Government of the United States:

NOW, THEREFORE, by virtue of the power vested in me by the Constitution and laws of the United States, particularly by the Joint Resolution approved June 22, 1942, as amended by the Joint Resolution approved December 22, 1942 [now sections 4 to 10 of this title], as President and Commander in Chief, it is hereby proclaimed as follows:

1. The use of the flag of the United States or any representation thereof, if approved by the Foreign Economic Administration, on labels, packages, cartons, cases, or other containers for articles or products of the United States intended for export as lend-lease aid, or relief and rehabilitation aid, or as emergency supplies for the Territories and possessions of the United States, or similar purposes, shall be considered a proper use of the flag of the United States and consistent with the honor and respect due to the flag.

2. If any article or product so labelled, packaged or otherwise bearing the flag of the United States or any representation thereof, as provided for in section 1, should, by force of circumstances, be diverted to the ordinary channels of domestic trade, no person shall be

considered as violating the rules and customs pertaining to the display of the flag of the United States, as set forth in the Joint Resolution approved June 22, 1942, as amended by the Joint Resolution approved December 22, 1942 (U.S.C., Supp. II, title 36, secs. 171–178) [now sections 4 to 10 of this title] for possessing, transporting, displaying, selling or otherwise transferring any such article or product solely because the label, package, carton, case, or other container bears the flag of the United States or any representation thereof.

CHAPTER 2—THE SEAL

Sec.
41.   Seal of the United States.
42.   Same; custody and use of.

§ 41. Seal of the United States

The seal heretofore used by the United States in Congress assembled is declared to be the seal of the United States.

(July 30, 1947, ch. 389, 61 Stat. 643.)

§ 42. Same; custody and use of

The Secretary of State shall have the custody and charge of such seal. Except as provided by section 2902(a) of title 5, the seal shall not be affixed to any instrument without the special warrant of the President therefor.

(July 30, 1947, ch. 389, 61 Stat. 643; Pub. L. 89–554, § 2(a), Sept. 6, 1966, 80 Stat. 608.)

AMENDMENTS

1966—Pub. L. 89–554 struck out provisions which required the Secretary of State to make out and record, and to affix the seal to, all civil commissions for officers of the United States appointed by the President. See section 2902(a) of Title 5, Government Organization and Employees.

Ex. ORD. NO. 10347. AFFIXING OF SEAL WITHOUT SPECIAL WARRANT

Ex. Ord. No. 10347, Apr. 18, 1952, 17 F.R. 3521, as amended by Ex. Ord. No. 11354, May 23, 1967, 32 F.R. 7695; Ex. Ord. No. 11517, Mar. 19, 1970, 35 F.R. 4937, provided:

By virtue of the authority vested in me by section 301 of title 3 of the United States Code (section 10, Public Law 248, approved October 31, 1951, 65 Stat. 713), and as President of the United States, I hereby authorize and direct the Secretary of State to affix the Seal of the United States, pursuant to section 42 of title 4 of the United States Code [this section], without any special warrant therefor, other than this order, to each document included within any of the following classes of documents when such document has been signed by the President and, in the case of any such document to which the counter-signature of the Secretary of State is required to be affixed, has been counter-signed by the said Secretary:

1. Proclamations by the President of treaties, conventions, protocols, or other international agreements.
2. Instruments of ratification of treaties.
3. Full powers to negotiate treaties and to exchange ratifications.
4. Letters of credence and recall and other communications from the President to heads of foreign governments.
5. Exequaturs issued to those foreign consular officers in the United States whose commissions bear the signature of the chief of state which they represent.

CHAPTER 3—SEAT OF THE GOVERNMENT

Sec.
71.   Permanent seat of Government.

72.   Public offices; at seat of Government.
73.   Same; removal from seat of Government.

§ 71. Permanent seat of Government

All that part of the territory of the United States included within the present limits of the District of Columbia shall be the permanent seat of government of the United States.

(July 30, 1947, ch. 389, 61 Stat. 643.)

§ 72. Public offices; at seat of Government

All offices attached to the seat of government shall be exercised in the District of Columbia, and not elsewhere, except as otherwise expressly provided by law.

(July 30, 1947, ch. 389, 61 Stat. 643.)

§ 73. Same; removal from seat of Government

In case of the prevalence of a contagious or epidemic disease at the seat of government, the President may permit and direct the removal of any or all the public offices to such other place or places as he shall deem most safe and convenient for conducting the public business.

(July 30, 1947, ch. 389, 61 Stat. 643.)

CHAPTER 4—THE STATES

Sec.
101.   Oath by members of legislatures and officers.
102.   Same; by whom administered.
103.   Assent to purchase of lands for forts.
104.   Tax on motor fuel sold on military or other reservation; reports to State taxing authority.
105.   State, etc., taxation affecting Federal areas; sales or use tax.[1]
106.   Same; income tax.
107.   Same; exception of United States, its instrumentalities, and authorized purchasers therefrom.
108.   Same; jurisdiction of United States over Federal areas unaffected.
109.   Same; exception of Indians.
110.   Same; definitions.
111.   Same; taxation affecting Federal employees; income tax.
112.   Compacts between States for cooperation in prevention of crime; consent of Congress.
113.   Residence of Members of Congress for State income tax laws.
114.   Limitation on State income taxation of certain pension income[2]
115.   Limitation on State authority to tax compensation paid to individuals performing services at Fort Campbell, Kentucky.
116.   Rules for determining State and local government treatment of charges related to mobile telecommunications services.
117.   Sourcing rules.
118.   Limitations.
119.   Electronic databases for nationwide standard numeric jurisdictional codes.
120.   Procedure if no electronic database provided.
121.   Correction of erroneous data for place of primary use.
122.   Determination of place of primary use.
123.   Scope; special rules.
124.   Definitions.
125.   Nonseverability.

[1] So in original. Does not conform to section catchline.
[2] So in original. Probably should be followed by a period.

126.   No inference.

AMENDMENTS

2000—Pub. L. 106–252, §2(b), July 28, 2000, 114 Stat. 633, added items 116 to 126.

1998—Pub. L. 105–261, div. A, title X, §1075(a)(2), Oct. 17, 1998, 112 Stat. 2138, added item 115.

1996—Pub. L. 104–95, §1(b), Jan. 10, 1996, 109 Stat. 980, added item 114.

1977—Pub. L. 95–67, §1(b), July 19, 1977, 91 Stat. 271, added item 113.

1966—Pub. L. 89–554, §2(b), Sept. 6, 1966, 80 Stat. 608, added item 111 and redesignated former item 111 as 112.

1949—Act May 24, 1949, ch. 139, §129(a), 63 Stat. 107, added item 111.

CIVIL AND CRIMINAL JURISDICTION OVER INDIANS

Amendment of State Constitutions to remove legal impediment to the assumption of civil and criminal jurisdiction in accordance with the provisions of section 1162 of Title 18 and section 1360 of Title 28, see act Aug. 15, 1953, ch. 505, §6, 67 Stat. 590, set out as a note under section 1360 of Title 28, Judiciary and Judicial Procedure.

Consent of United States to other States to assume jurisdiction with respect to criminal offenses or civil causes of action, or with respect to both, as provided for in section 1162 of Title 18 and section 1360 of Title 28, see act Aug. 15, 1953, ch. 505, §7, 67 Stat. 590, set out as a note under section 1360 of Title 28.

§ 101. Oath by members of legislatures and officers

Every member of a State legislature, and every executive and judicial officer of a State, shall, before he proceeds to execute the duties of his office, take an oath in the following form, to wit: "I, A B, do solemnly swear that I will support the Constitution of the United States."

(July 30, 1947, ch. 389, 61 Stat. 643.)

§ 102. Same; by whom administered

Such oath may be administered by any person who, by the law of the State, is authorized to administer the oath of office; and the person so administering such oath shall cause a record or certificate thereof to be made in the same manner, as by the law of the State, he is directed to record or certify the oath of office.

(July 30, 1947, ch. 389, 61 Stat. 644.)

§ 103. Assent to purchase of lands for forts

The President of the United States is authorized to procure the assent of the legislature of any State, within which any purchase of land has been made for the erection of forts, magazines, arsenals, dockyards, and other needful buildings, without such consent having been obtained.

(July 30, 1947, ch. 389, 61 Stat. 644.)

§ 104. Tax on motor fuel sold on military or other reservation[1] reports to State taxing authority

(a) All taxes levied by any State, Territory, or the District of Columbia upon, with respect to, or measured by, sales, purchases, storage, or use of gasoline or other motor vehicle fuels may be levied, in the same manner and to the same ex-

tent, with respect to such fuels when sold by or through post exchanges, ship stores, ship service stores, commissaries, filling stations, licensed traders, and other similar agencies, located on United States military or other reservations, when such fuels are not for the exclusive use of the United States. Such taxes, so levied, shall be paid to the proper taxing authorities of the State, Territory, or the District of Columbia, within whose borders the reservation affected may be located.

(b) The officer in charge of such reservation shall, on or before the fifteenth day of each month, submit a written statement to the proper taxing authorities of the State, Territory, or the District of Columbia within whose borders the reservation is located, showing the amount of such motor fuel with respect to which taxes are payable under subsection (a) for the preceding month.

(c) As used in this section, the term "Territory" shall include Guam.

(July 30, 1947, ch. 389, 61 Stat. 644; Aug. 1, 1956, ch. 827, 70 Stat. 799.)

AMENDMENTS

1956—Subsec. (c) added by act Aug. 1, 1956.

CIVIL AIRPORTS OWNED BY UNITED STATES SUBJECT TO SECTIONS 104 TO 110; SALES OR USE TAXES: FUELS FOR AIRCRAFT OR OTHER SERVICING OF AIRCRAFT; LANDING OR TAKING OFF CHARGES; LEASES

Section 210 of Pub. L. 91–258, title II, May 21, 1970, 84 Stat. 253, provided that:

"(a) Nothing in this title or in any other law of the United States shall prevent the application of sections 104 through 110 of title 4 of the United States Code to civil airports owned by the United States.

"(b) Subsection (a) shall not apply to—

"(1) sales or use taxes in respect of fuels for aircraft or in respect of other servicing of aircraft, or

"(2) taxes, fees, head charges, or other charges in respect of the landing or taking off of aircraft or aircraft passengers or freight.

"(c) In the case of any lease in effect on September 28, 1969, subsection (a) shall not authorize the levy or collection of any tax in respect of any transaction occurring, or any service performed, pursuant to such lease before the expiration of such lease (determined without regard to any renewal or extension of such lease made after September 28, 1969). For purposes of the preceding sentence, the term 'lease' includes a contract."

§ 105. State, and so forth, taxation affecting Federal areas; sales or use tax

(a) No person shall be relieved from liability for payment of, collection of, or accounting for any sales or use tax levied by any State, or by any duly constituted taxing authority therein, having jurisdiction to levy such a tax, on the ground that the sale or use, with respect to which such tax is levied, occurred in whole or in part within a Federal area; and such State or taxing authority shall have full jurisdiction and power to levy and collect any such tax in any Federal area within such State to the same extent and with the same effect as though such area was not a Federal area.

(b) The provisions of subsection (a) shall be applicable only with respect to sales or purchases made, receipts from sales received, or storage or use occurring, after December 31, 1940.

---

[1] So in original. Probably should be followed by a semicolon.

(July 30, 1947, ch. 389, 61 Stat. 644.)

TAXATION WITH RESPECT TO ESSENTIAL SUPPORT ACTIVITIES OR FUNCTIONS OF NON-GOVERNMENTAL PERSONS IN CONGRESSIONALLY-CONTROLLED LOCATIONS IN DISTRICT OF COLUMBIA

Pub. L. 100–202, § 101(i) [title III, § 307], Dec. 22, 1987, 101 Stat. 1329–290, 1329–309, as amended by Pub. L. 104–186, title II, § 214, Aug. 20, 1996, 110 Stat. 1745, provided that:

"(a) Notwithstanding section 105 of title 4, United States Code, or any other provision of law, no person shall be required to pay, collect, or account for any sales, use, or similar excise tax, or any personal property tax, with respect to an essential support activity or function conducted by a nongovernmental person in the Capitol, the House Office Buildings, the Senate Office Buildings, the Capitol Grounds, or any other location under the control of the Congress in the District of Columbia.

"(b) As used in this section—

"(1) the term 'essential support activity or function' means a support activity or function so designated by the Committee on House Oversight [now Committee on House Administration] of the House of Representatives or the Committee on Rules and Administration of the Senate, acting jointly or separately, as appropriate;

"(2) the term 'personal property tax' means a tax of a State, a subdivision of a State, or any other authority of a State, that is levied on, levied with respect to, or measured by, the value of personal property;

"(3) the term 'sales, use, or similar excise tax' means a tax of a State, a subdivision of a State, or any other authority of a State, that is levied on, levied with respect to, or measured by, sales, receipts from sales, or purchases, or by storage, possession, or use of personal property; and

"(4) the term 'State' means a State of the United States, the District of Columbia, or a territory or possession of the United States.

"(c) This section shall apply to any sale, receipt, purchase, storage, possession, use, or valuation taking place after December 31, 1986."

§ 106. Same; income tax

(a) No person shall be relieved from liability for any income tax levied by any State, or by any duly constituted taxing authority therein, having jurisdiction to levy such a tax, by reason of his residing within a Federal area or receiving income from transactions occurring or services performed in such area; and such State or taxing authority shall have full jurisdiction and power to levy and collect such tax in any Federal area within such State to the same extent and with the same effect as though such area was not a Federal area.

(b) The provisions of subsection (a) shall be applicable only with respect to income or receipts received after December 31, 1940.

(July 30, 1947, ch. 389, 61 Stat. 644.)

§ 107. Same; exception of United States, its instrumentalities, and authorized purchases [1] therefrom

(a) The provisions of sections 105 and 106 of this title shall not be deemed to authorize the levy or collection of any tax on or from the United States or any instrumentality thereof, or the levy or collection of any tax with respect to sale, purchase, storage, or use of tangible per-

---

[1] So in original. Probably should be "purchasers".

---

sonal property sold by the United States or any instrumentality thereof to any authorized purchaser.

(b) A person shall be deemed to be an authorized purchaser under this section only with respect to purchases which he is permitted to make from commissaries, ship's stores, or voluntary unincorporated organizations of personnel of any branch of the Armed Forces of the United States, under regulations promulgated by the departmental Secretary having jurisdiction over such branch.

(July 30, 1947, ch. 389, 61 Stat. 645; Sept. 3, 1954, ch. 1263, § 4, 68 Stat. 1227.)

AMENDMENTS

1954—Subsec. (b). Act Sept. 3, 1954, substituted "personnel of any branch of the Armed Forces of the United States" for "Army or Navy personnel".

§ 108. Same; jurisdiction of United States over Federal areas unaffected

The provisions of sections 105–110 of this title shall not for the purposes of any other provision of law be deemed to deprive the United States of exclusive jurisdiction over any Federal area over which it would otherwise have exclusive jurisdiction or to limit the jurisdiction of the United States over any Federal area.

(July 30, 1947, ch. 389, 61 Stat. 645.)

§ 109. Same; exception of Indians

Nothing in sections 105 and 106 of this title shall be deemed to authorize the levy or collection of any tax on or from any Indian not otherwise taxed.

(July 30, 1947, ch. 389, 61 Stat. 645.)

§ 110. Same; definitions

As used in sections 105–109 of this title—

(a) The term "person" shall have the meaning assigned to it in section 3797 of title 26.

(b) The term "sales or use tax" means any tax levied on, with respect to, or measured by, sales, receipts from sales, purchases, storage, or use of tangible personal property, except a tax with respect to which the provisions of section 104 of this title are applicable.

(c) The term "income tax" means any tax levied on, with respect to, or measured by, net income, gross income, or gross receipts.

(d) The term "State" includes any Territory or possession of the United States.

(e) The term "Federal area" means any lands or premises held or acquired by or for the use of the United States or any department, establishment, or agency, of the United States; and any Federal area, or any part thereof, which is located within the exterior boundaries of any State, shall be deemed to be a Federal area located within such State.

(July 30, 1947, ch. 389, 61 Stat. 645.)

REFERENCES IN TEXT

Section 3797 of title 26, referred to in subsec. (a), is a reference to section 3797 of the Internal Revenue Code of 1939, which was repealed by section 7851 of the Internal Revenue Code of 1954, Title 26, and is covered by section 7701(a)(1) of Title 26. The Internal Revenue Code of 1954 was redesignated the Internal Revenue Code of 1986 by Pub. L. 99–514, § 2, Oct. 22, 1986, 100 Stat. 2095. For table of comparisons of the 1939 Code to the 1986 Code, see Table I preceding section 1 of Title 26, Internal Revenue Code. See also section 7852(b) of Title 26, Internal Revenue Code, for provision that references in any other law to a provision of the 1939 Code, unless expressly incompatible with the intent thereof, shall be deemed a reference to the corresponding provision of the 1986 Code.

§ 111. Same; taxation affecting Federal employees; income tax

(a) GENERAL RULE.—The United States consents to the taxation of pay or compensation for personal service as an officer or employee of the United States, a territory or possession or political subdivision thereof, the government of the District of Columbia, or an agency or instrumentality of one or more of the foregoing, by a duly constituted taxing authority having jurisdiction, if the taxation does not discriminate against the officer or employee because of the source of the pay or compensation.

(b) TREATMENT OF CERTAIN FEDERAL EMPLOYEES EMPLOYED AT FEDERAL HYDROELECTRIC FACILITIES LOCATED ON THE COLUMBIA RIVER.—Pay or compensation paid by the United States for personal services as an employee of the United States at a hydroelectric facility—

(1) which is owned by the United States;
(2) which is located on the Columbia River; and
(3) portions of which are within the States of Oregon and Washington,

shall be subject to taxation by the State or any political subdivision thereof of which such employee is a resident.

(c) TREATMENT OF CERTAIN FEDERAL EMPLOYEES EMPLOYED AT FEDERAL HYDROELECTRIC FACILITIES LOCATED ON THE MISSOURI RIVER.—Pay or compensation paid by the United States for personal services as an employee of the United States at a hydroelectric facility—

(1) which is owned by the United States;
(2) which is located on the Missouri River; and
(3) portions of which are within the States of South Dakota and Nebraska,

shall be subject to taxation by the State or any political subdivision thereof of which such employee is a resident.

(Added Pub. L. 89–554, § 2(c), Sept. 6, 1966, 80 Stat. 608; amended Pub. L. 105–261, div. A, title X, § 1075(b)(1), Oct. 17, 1998, 112 Stat. 2138.)

HISTORICAL AND REVISION NOTES

Derivation	U.S. Code	Revised Statutes and Statutes at Large
....	5 U.S.C. 84a ...	Apr. 12, 1939, ch. 59, § 4, 53 Stat. 575.

The words "received after December 31, 1938," are omitted as obsolete. The words "pay or" are added before "compensation" for clarity as the word "pay" is used throughout title 5, United States Code, to refer to the remuneration, salary, wages, or compensation for the personal services of a Federal employee. The word "territory" is not capitalized as there are no longer any "Territories." The words "to tax such compensation" are omitted as unnecessary.

AMENDMENTS

1998—Pub. L. 105–261 designated existing provisions as subsec. (a), inserted heading, and added subsecs. (b) and (c).

EFFECTIVE DATE OF 1998 AMENDMENT

Pub. L. 105–261, div. A, title X, § 1075(b)(2), Oct. 17, 1998, 112 Stat. 2139, provided that: "The amendment made by this subsection [amending this section] shall apply to pay and compensation paid after the date of the enactment of this Act [Oct. 17, 1998]."

§ 112. Compacts between States for cooperation in prevention of crime; consent of Congress

(a) The consent of Congress is hereby given to any two or more States to enter into agreements or compacts for cooperative effort and mutual assistance in the prevention of crime and in the enforcement of their respective criminal laws and policies, and to establish such agencies, joint or otherwise, as they may deem desirable for making effective such agreements and compacts.

(b) For the purpose of this section, the term "States" means the several States and Alaska, Hawaii, the Commonwealth of Puerto Rico, the Virgin Islands, Guam, and the District of Columbia.

(Added May 24, 1949, ch. 139, § 129(b), 63 Stat. 107, § 112, formerly § 111; amended Aug. 3, 1956, ch. 941, 70 Stat. 1020; Pub. L. 87–406, Feb. 16, 1962, 76 Stat. 9; renumbered § 112, Pub. L. 89–554, § 2(c), Sept. 6, 1966, 80 Stat. 608.)

HISTORICAL AND REVISION NOTE

This section [section 129(b) of Act May 24, 1949] incorporates in title 4, U.S.C. (enacted into positive law by act of July 30, 1947 (ch. 389, § 1, 61 Stat. 641), the provisions of former section 420 of title 18, U.S.C. (act of June 6, 1934, ch. 406, 48 Stat. 909), which, in the course of the revision of such title 18, was omitted therefrom and recommended for transfer to such title 4. (See table 7—Transferred sections, p. A219, H. Rept. No. 304, April 24, 1947, to accompany H.R. 3190, 80th Cong.).

AMENDMENTS

1962—Subsec. (b). Pub. L. 87–406 inserted "Guam" after "the Virgin Islands,".

1956—Act Aug. 3, 1956, designated existing provisions as subsec. (a) and added subsec. (b).

ADMISSION OF ALASKA AND HAWAII TO STATEHOOD

Alaska was admitted into the Union on Jan. 3, 1959, on issuance of Proc. No. 3269, Jan. 3, 1959, 24 F.R. 81, 73 Stat. c16, and Hawaii was admitted into the Union on Aug. 21, 1959, on issuance of Proc. No. 3309, Aug. 21, 1959, 24 F.R. 6868, 73 Stat. c74. For Alaska Statehood Law, see Pub. L. 85–508, July 7, 1958, 72 Stat. 339, set out as a note preceding former section 21 of Title 48, Territories and Insular Possessions. For Hawaii Statehood Law, see Pub. L. 86–3, Mar. 18, 1959, 73 Stat. 4, set out as a note preceding former section 491 of Title 48.

§ 113. Residence of Members of Congress for State income tax laws

(a) No State, or political subdivision thereof, in which a Member of Congress maintains a place of abode for purposes of attending sessions of Congress may, for purposes of any income tax (as defined in section 110(c) of this title) levied by such State or political subdivision thereof—

(1) treat such Member as a resident or domiciliary of such State or political subdivision thereof; or

(2) treat any compensation paid by the United States to such Member as income for services performed within, or from sources within, such State or political subdivision thereof,

unless such Member represents such State or a district in such State.

(b) For purposes of subsection (a)—

(1) the term "Member of Congress" includes the delegates from the District of Columbia, Guam, and the Virgin Islands, and the Resident Commissioner from Puerto Rico; and

(2) the term "State" includes the District of Columbia.

(Added Pub. L. 95–67, § 1(a), July 19, 1977, 91 Stat. 271.)

EFFECTIVE DATE

Section 1(c) of Pub. L. 95–67 provided that: "The amendments made by subsections (a) and (b) [enacting this section and amending analysis preceding section 101 of this title] shall be effective with respect to all taxable years, whether beginning before, on, or after the date of the enactment of this Act [July 19, 1977]."

RESIDENCE OF MEMBERS OF CONGRESS FOR STATE PERSONAL PROPERTY TAX ON MOTOR VEHICLES

Pub. L. 99–190, § 101(c) [H.R. 3067, § 131], Dec. 19, 1985, 99 Stat. 1224; Pub. L. 100–202, § 106, Dec. 22, 1987, 101 Stat. 1329–433, provided that:

"(a) No State, or political subdivision thereof, in which a Member of Congress maintains a place of abode for purposes of attending sessions of Congress may impose a personal property tax with respect to any motor vehicle owned by such Member (or by the spouse of such Member) unless such Member represents such State or a district in such State.

"(b) For purposes of this section—

"(1) the term 'Member of Congress' includes the delegates from the District of Columbia, Guam, and the Virgin Islands, and the Resident Commissioner from Puerto Rico;

"(2) the term 'State' includes the District of Columbia; and

"(3) the term 'personal property tax' means any tax imposed on an annual basis and levied on, with respect to, or measured by, the market value or assessed value of an item of personal property.

"(c) This section shall apply to all taxable periods beginning on or after January 1, 1985."

§ 114. Limitation on State income taxation of certain pension income

(a) No State may impose an income tax on any retirement income of an individual who is not a resident or domiciliary of such State (as determined under the laws of such State).

(b) For purposes of this section—

(1) The term "retirement income" means any income from—

(A) a qualified trust under section 401(a) of the Internal Revenue Code of 1986 that is exempt under section 501(a) from taxation;

(B) a simplified employee pension as defined in section 408(k) of such Code;

(C) an annuity plan described in section 403(a) of such Code;

(D) an annuity contract described in section 403(b) of such Code;

(E) an individual retirement plan described in section 7701(a)(37) of such Code;

(F) an eligible deferred compensation plan (as defined in section 457 of such Code);

(G) a governmental plan (as defined in section 414(d) of such Code);

(H) a trust described in section 501(c)(18) of such Code; or

(I) any plan, program, or arrangement described in section 3121(v)(2)(C) of such Code (or any plan, program, or arrangement that is in writing, that provides for retirement payments in recognition of prior service to be made to a retired partner, and that is in effect immediately before retirement begins), if such income—

(i) is part of a series of substantially equal periodic payments (not less frequently than annually which may include income described in subparagraphs (A) through (H)) made for—

(I) the life or life expectancy of the recipient (or the joint lives or joint life expectancies of the recipient and the designated beneficiary of the recipient), or

(II) a period of not less than 10 years, or

(ii) is a payment received after termination of employment and under a plan, program, or arrangement (to which such employment relates) maintained solely for the purpose of providing retirement benefits for employees in excess of the limitations imposed by 1 or more of sections 401(a)(17), 401(k), 401(m), 402(g), 403(b), 408(k), or 415 of such Code or any other limitation on contributions or benefits in such Code on plans to which any of such sections apply.

The fact that payments may be adjusted from time to time pursuant to such plan, program, or arrangement to limit total disbursements under a predetermined formula, or to provide cost of living or similar adjustments, will not cause the periodic payments provided under such plan, program, or arrangement to fail the "substantially equal periodic payments" test.

Such term includes any retired or retainer pay of a member or former member of a uniform service computed under chapter 71 of title 10, United States Code.

(2) The term "income tax" has the meaning given such term by section 110(c).

(3) The term "State" includes any political subdivision of a State, the District of Columbia, and the possessions of the United States.

(4) For purposes of this section, the term "retired partner" is an individual who is described as a partner in section 7701(a)(2) of the Internal Revenue Code of 1986 and who is retired under such individual's partnership agreement.

(e)[1] Nothing in this section shall be construed as having any effect on the application of section 514 of the Employee Retirement Income Security Act of 1974.

(Added Pub. L. 104–95, § 1(a), Jan. 10, 1996, 109 Stat. 979; amended Pub. L. 109–264, § 1(a), Aug. 3, 2006, 120 Stat. 667.)

[1] So in original. No subsecs. (c) and (d) have been enacted.

REFERENCES IN TEXT

The Internal Revenue Code of 1986, referred to in subsec. (b)(1), (4), is classified generally to Title 26, Internal Revenue Code.

Section 514 of the Employee Retirement Income Security Act of 1974, referred to in subsec. (e), is classified to section 1144 of Title 29, Labor.

AMENDMENTS

2006—Subsec. (b)(1)(I). Pub. L. 109–264, § 1(a)(1)–(3), inserted "(or any plan, program, or arrangement that is in writing, that provides for retirement payments in recognition of prior service to be made to a retired partner, and that is in effect immediately before retirement begins)" after "section 3121(v)(2)(C) of such Code" in introductory provisions, "which may include income described in subparagraphs (A) through (H)" after "(not less frequently than annually)" in cl. (1), and concluding provisions at end.

Subsec. (b)(4). Pub. L. 109–264, § 1(a)(4), which directed the addition of par. (4) at end of subsec. (b)(1)(I), was executed by adding par. (4) at end of subsec. (b) to reflect the probable intent of Congress.

EFFECTIVE DATE OF 2006 AMENDMENT

Pub. L. 109–264, § 1(b), Aug. 3, 2006, 120 Stat. 667, provided that: "The amendments made by this section [amending this section] apply to amounts received after December 31, 1995."

EFFECTIVE DATE

Section 1(c) of Pub. L. 104–95 provided that: "The amendments made by this section [enacting this section] shall apply to amounts received after December 31, 1995."

§ 115. Limitation on State authority to tax compensation paid to individuals performing services at Fort Campbell, Kentucky

Pay and compensation paid to an individual for personal services at Fort Campbell, Kentucky, shall be subject to taxation by the State or any political subdivision thereof of which such employee is a resident.

(Added Pub. L. 105–261, div. A, title X, § 1075(a)(1), Oct. 17, 1998, 112 Stat. 2138.)

EFFECTIVE DATE

Pub. L. 105–261, div. A, title X, § 1075(a)(3), Oct. 17, 1998, 112 Stat. 2138, provided that: "The amendments made by this subsection [enacting this section] apply to pay and compensation paid after the date of the enactment of this Act [Oct. 17, 1998]."

§ 116. Rules for determining State and local government treatment of charges related to mobile telecommunications services

(a) APPLICATION OF THIS SECTION THROUGH SECTION 126.—This section through[1] 126 of this title apply to any tax, charge, or fee levied by a taxing jurisdiction as a fixed charge for each customer or measured by gross amounts charged to customers for mobile telecommunications services, regardless of whether such tax, charge, or fee is imposed on the vendor or customer of the service and regardless of the terminology used to describe the tax, charge, or fee.

(b) GENERAL EXCEPTIONS.—This section through[1] 126 of this title do not apply to—

(1) any tax, charge, or fee levied upon or measured by the net income, capital stock,

net worth, or property value of the provider of mobile telecommunications service;

(2) any tax, charge, or fee that is applied to an equitably apportioned amount that is not determined on a transactional basis;

(3) any tax, charge, or fee that represents compensation for a mobile telecommunications service provider's use of public rights of way or other public property, provided that such tax, charge, or fee is not levied by the taxing jurisdiction as a fixed charge for each customer or measured by gross amounts charged to customers for mobile telecommunication services;

(4) any generally applicable business and occupation tax that is imposed by a State, is applied to gross receipts or gross proceeds, is the legal liability of the home service provider, and that statutorily allows the home service provider to elect to use the sourcing method required in this section through[1] 126 of this title;

(5) any fee related to obligations under section 254 of the Communications Act of 1934; or

(6) any tax, charge, or fee imposed by the Federal Communications Commission.

(c) SPECIFIC EXCEPTIONS.—This section through[1] 126 of this title—

(1) do not apply to the determination of the taxing situs of prepaid telephone calling services;

(2) do not affect the taxability of either the initial sale of mobile telecommunications services or subsequent resale of such services, whether as sales of such services alone or as a part of a bundled product, if the Internet Tax Freedom Act would preclude a taxing jurisdiction from subjecting the charges of the sale of such services to a tax, charge, or fee, but this section provides no evidence of the intent of Congress with respect to the applicability of the Internet Tax Freedom Act to such charges; and

(3) do not apply to the determination of the taxing situs of air-ground radiotelephone service as defined in section 22.99 of title 47 of the Code of Federal Regulations as in effect on June 1, 1999.

(Added Pub. L. 106–252, § 2(a), July 28, 2000, 114 Stat. 626.)

REFERENCES IN TEXT

Section 254 of the Communications Act of 1934, referred to in subsec. (b)(5), is classified to section 254 of Title 47, Telegraphs, Telephones, and Radiotelegraphs.

The Internet Tax Freedom Act, referred to in subsec. (c)(2), is title XI of Pub. L. 105–277, div. C, Oct. 21, 1998, 112 Stat. 2681–719, which is set out as a note under section 151 of Title 47, Telegraphs, Telephones, and Radiotelegraphs.

EFFECTIVE DATE; APPLICATION OF AMENDMENT

Pub. L. 106–252, § 3, July 28, 2000, 114 Stat. 633, provided that:

"(a) EFFECTIVE DATE.—Except as provided in subsection (b), this Act [enacting this section and sections 117 to 126 of this title and provisions set out as a note under section 1 of this title] and the amendment made by this Act shall take effect on the date of the enactment of this Act [July 28, 2000].

"(b) APPLICATION OF ACT.—The amendment made by this Act [enacting this section and sections 117 to 126 of

---

[1] So in original. Probably should be followed by "section".

this title] shall apply only to customer bills issued after the first day of the first month beginning more than 2 years after the date of the enactment of this Act [July 28, 2000].''

§ 117. Sourcing rules

(a) TREATMENT OF CHARGES FOR MOBILE TELE-COMMUNICATIONS SERVICES.—Notwithstanding the law of any State or political subdivision of any State, mobile telecommunications services provided in a taxing jurisdiction to a customer, the charges for which are billed by or for the customer's home service provider, shall be deemed to be provided by the customer's home service provider.

(b) JURISDICTION.—All charges for mobile tele-communications services that are deemed to be provided by the customer's home service provider under sections 116 through 126 of this title are authorized to be subjected to tax, charge, or fee by the taxing jurisdictions whose territorial limits encompass the customer's place of primary use, regardless of where the mobile telecommunication services originate, terminate, or pass through, and no other taxing jurisdiction may impose taxes, charges, or fees on charges for such mobile telecommunications services.

(Added Pub. L. 106–252, § 2(a), July 28, 2000, 114 Stat. 627.)

EFFECTIVE DATE; APPLICATION OF AMENDMENT

Section effective July 28, 2000, and applicable only to customer bills issued after the first day of the first month beginning more than 2 years after July 28, 2000, see section 3 of Pub. L. 106–252, set out as a note under section 116 of this title.

§ 118. Limitations

Sections 116 through 126 of this title do not—
  (1) provide authority to a taxing jurisdiction to impose a tax, charge, or fee that the laws of such jurisdiction do not authorize such jurisdiction to impose; or
  (2) modify, impair, supersede, or authorize the modification, impairment, or supersession of the law of any taxing jurisdiction pertaining to taxation except as expressly provided in sections 116 through 126 of this title.

(Added Pub. L. 106–252, § 2(a), July 28, 2000, 114 Stat. 627.)

EFFECTIVE DATE; APPLICATION OF AMENDMENT

Section effective July 28, 2000, and applicable only to customer bills issued after the first day of the first month beginning more than 2 years after July 28, 2000, see section 3 of Pub. L. 106–252, set out as a note under section 116 of this title.

§ 119. Electronic databases for nationwide standard numeric jurisdictional codes

(a) ELECTRONIC DATABASE.—
  (1) PROVISION OF DATABASE.—A State may provide an electronic database to a home service provider or, if a State does not provide such an electronic database to home service providers, then the designated database provider may provide an electronic database to a home service provider.
  (2) FORMAT.—(A) Such electronic database, whether provided by the State or the designated database provider, shall be provided in

a format approved by the American National Standards Institute's Accredited Standards Committee X12, that, allowing for de minimis deviations, designates for each street address in the State, including to the extent practicable, any multiple postal street addresses applicable to one street location, the appropriate taxing jurisdictions, and the appropriate code for each taxing jurisdiction, for each level of taxing jurisdiction, identified by one nationwide standard numeric code.

(B) Such electronic database shall also provide the appropriate code for each street address with respect to political subdivisions which are not taxing jurisdictions when reasonably needed to determine the proper taxing jurisdiction.

(C) The nationwide standard numeric codes shall contain the same number of numeric digits with each digit or combination of digits referring to the same level of taxing jurisdiction throughout the United States using a format similar to FIPS 55–3 or other appropriate standard approved by the Federation of Tax Administrators and the Multistate Tax Commission, or their successors. Each address shall be provided in standard postal format.

(b) NOTICE; UPDATES.—A State or designated database provider that provides or maintains an electronic database described in subsection (a) shall provide notice of the availability of the then current electronic database, and any subsequent revisions thereof, by publication in the manner normally employed for the publication of informational tax, charge, or fee notices to taxpayers in such State.

(c) USER HELD HARMLESS.—A home service provider using the data contained in an electronic database described in subsection (a) shall be held harmless from any tax, charge, or fee liability that otherwise would be due solely as a result of any error or omission in such database provided by a State or designated database provider. The home service provider shall reflect changes made to such database during a calendar quarter not later than 30 days after the end of such calendar quarter for each State that issues notice of the availability of an electronic database reflecting such changes under subsection (b).

(Added Pub. L. 106–252, § 2(a), July 28, 2000, 114 Stat. 627.)

EFFECTIVE DATE; APPLICATION OF AMENDMENT

Section effective July 28, 2000, and applicable only to customer bills issued after the first day of the first month beginning more than 2 years after July 28, 2000, see section 3 of Pub. L. 106–252, set out as a note under section 116 of this title.

§ 120. Procedure if no electronic database provided

(a) SAFE HARBOR.—If neither a State nor designated database provider provides an electronic database under section 119, a home service provider shall be held harmless from any tax, charge, or fee liability in such State that otherwise would be due solely as a result of an assignment of a street address to an incorrect taxing jurisdiction if, subject to section 121, the home service provider employs an enhanced zip code to assign each street address to a specific taxing jurisdiction for each level of taxing jurisdiction and exercises due diligence at each level of taxing jurisdiction to ensure that each such street address is assigned to the correct taxing jurisdiction. If an enhanced zip code overlaps boundaries of taxing jurisdictions of the same level, the home service provider must designate one specific jurisdiction within such enhanced zip code for use in taxing the activity for such enhanced zip code for each level of taxing jurisdiction. Any enhanced zip code assignment changed in accordance with section 121 is deemed to be in compliance with this section. For purposes of this section, there is a rebuttable presumption that a home service provider has exercised due diligence if such home service provider demonstrates that it has—

(1) expended reasonable resources to implement and maintain an appropriately detailed electronic database of street address assignments to taxing jurisdictions;

(2) implemented and maintained reasonable internal controls to promptly correct misassignments of street addresses to taxing jurisdictions; and

(3) used all reasonably obtainable and usable data pertaining to municipal annexations, incorporations, reorganizations and any other changes in jurisdictional boundaries that materially affect the accuracy of such database.

(b) TERMINATION OF SAFE HARBOR.—Subsection (a) applies to a home service provider that is in compliance with the requirements of subsection (a), with respect to a State for which an electronic database is not provided under section 119 until the later of—

(1) 18 months after the nationwide standard numeric code described in section 119(a) has been approved by the Federation of Tax Administrators and the Multistate Tax Commission; or

(2) 6 months after such State or a designated database provider in such State provides such database as prescribed in section 119(a).

(Added Pub. L. 106–252, § 2(a), July 28, 2000, 114 Stat. 628.)

EFFECTIVE DATE; APPLICATION OF AMENDMENT

Section effective July 28, 2000, and applicable only to customer bills issued after the first day of the first month beginning more than 2 years after July 28, 2000, see section 3 of Pub. L. 106–252, set out as a note under section 116 of this title.

§ 121. Correction of erroneous data for place of primary use

(a)[1] IN GENERAL.—A taxing jurisdiction, or a State on behalf of any taxing jurisdiction or taxing jurisdictions within such State, may—

(1) determine that the address used for purposes of determining the taxing jurisdictions to which taxes, charges, or fees for mobile telecommunications services are remitted does not meet the definition of place of primary use in section 124(8) and give binding notice to the home service provider to change

---

[1] So in original. No subsec. (b) was enacted.

the place of primary use on a prospective basis from the date of notice of determination if—

(A) if the taxing jurisdiction making such determination is not a State, such taxing jurisdiction obtains the consent of all affected taxing jurisdictions within the State before giving such notice of determination; and

(B) before the taxing jurisdiction gives such notice of determination, the customer is given an opportunity to demonstrate in accordance with applicable State or local tax, charge, or fee administrative procedures that the address is the customer's place of primary use;

(2) determine that the assignment of a taxing jurisdiction by a home service provider under section 120 does not reflect the correct taxing jurisdiction and give binding notice to the home service provider to change the assignment on a prospective basis from the date of notice of determination if—

(A) if the taxing jurisdiction making such determination is not a State, such taxing jurisdiction obtains the consent of all affected taxing jurisdictions within the State before giving such notice of determination; and

(B) the home service provider is given an opportunity to demonstrate in accordance with applicable State or local tax, charge, or fee administrative procedures that the assignment reflects the correct taxing jurisdiction.

(Added Pub. L. 106–252, § 2(a), July 28, 2000, 114 Stat. 629.)

EFFECTIVE DATE; APPLICATION OF AMENDMENT

Section effective July 28, 2000, and applicable only to customer bills issued after the first day of the first month beginning more than 2 years after July 28, 2000, see section 3 of Pub. L. 106–252, set out as a note under section 116 of this title.

§ 122. Determination of place of primary use

(a) PLACE OF PRIMARY USE.—A home service provider shall be responsible for obtaining and maintaining the customer's place of primary use (as defined in section 124). Subject to section 121, and if the home service provider's reliance on information provided by its customer is in good faith, a taxing jurisdiction shall—

(1) allow a home service provider to rely on the applicable residential or business street address supplied by the home service provider's customer; and

(2) not hold a home service provider liable for any additional taxes, charges, or fees based on a different determination of the place of primary use for taxes, charges, or fees that are customarily passed on to the customer as a separate itemized charge.

(b) ADDRESS UNDER EXISTING AGREEMENTS.— Except as provided in section 121, a taxing jurisdiction shall allow a home service provider to treat the address used by the home service provider for tax purposes for any customer under a service contract or agreement in effect 2 years after the date of the enactment of the Mobile Telecommunications Sourcing Act as that customer's place of primary use for the remaining term of such service contract or agreement, excluding any extension or renewal of such service contract or agreement, for purposes of determining the taxing jurisdictions to which taxes, charges, or fees on charges for mobile telecommunications services are remitted.

(Added Pub. L. 106–252, § 2(a), July 28, 2000, 114 Stat. 630.)

REFERENCES IN TEXT

The date of the enactment of the Mobile Telecommunications Sourcing Act, referred to in subsec. (b), is the date of enactment of Pub. L. 106–252, which was approved July 28, 2000.

EFFECTIVE DATE; APPLICATION OF AMENDMENT

Section effective July 28, 2000, and applicable only to customer bills issued after the first day of the first month beginning more than 2 years after July 28, 2000, see section 3 of Pub. L. 106–252, set out as a note under section 116 of this title.

§ 123. Scope; special rules

(a) ACT DOES NOT SUPERSEDE CUSTOMER'S LIABILITY TO TAXING JURISDICTION.—Nothing in sections 116 through 126 modifies, impairs, supersedes, or authorizes the modification, impairment, or supersession of, any law allowing a taxing jurisdiction to collect a tax, charge, or fee from a customer that has failed to provide its place of primary use.

(b) ADDITIONAL TAXABLE CHARGES.—If a taxing jurisdiction does not otherwise subject charges for mobile telecommunications services to taxation and if these charges are aggregated with and not separately stated from charges that are subject to taxation, then the charges for nontaxable mobile telecommunications services may be subject to taxation unless the home service provider can reasonably identify charges not subject to such tax, charge, or fee from its books and records that are kept in the regular course of business.

(c) NONTAXABLE CHARGES.—If a taxing jurisdiction does not subject charges for mobile telecommunications services to taxation, a customer may not rely upon the nontaxability of charges for mobile telecommunications services unless the customer's home service provider separately states the charges for nontaxable mobile telecommunications services from taxable charges or the home service provider elects, after receiving a written request from the customer in the form required by the provider, to provide verifiable data based upon the home service provider's books and records that are kept in the regular course of business that reasonably identifies the nontaxable charges.

(Added Pub. L. 106–252, § 2(a), July 28, 2000, 114 Stat. 630.)

REFERENCES IN TEXT

Act, referred to in subsec. (a), probably means the Mobile Telecommunications Sourcing Act, Pub. L. 106–252, July 28, 2000, 114 Stat. 626, which enacted sections 116 to 126 of this title and provisions set out as notes under sections 1 and 116 of this title. For complete classification of this Act to the Code, see Short Title of 2000 Amendment note set out under section 1 of this title and Tables.

EFFECTIVE DATE; APPLICATION OF AMENDMENT

Section effective July 28, 2000, and applicable only to customer bills issued after the first day of the first month beginning more than 2 years after July 28, 2000, see section 3 of Pub. L. 106–252, set out as a note under section 116 of this title.

§ 124. Definitions

In sections 116 through 126 of this title:

(1) CHARGES FOR MOBILE TELECOMMUNICATIONS SERVICES.—The term "charges for mobile telecommunications services" means any charge for, or associated with, the provision of commercial mobile radio service, as defined in section 20.3 of title 47 of the Code of Federal Regulations as in effect on June 1, 1999, or any charge for, or associated with, a service provided as an adjunct to a commercial mobile radio service, that is billed to the customer by or for the customer's home service provider regardless of whether individual transmissions originate or terminate within the licensed service area of the home service provider.

(2) CUSTOMER.—

(A) IN GENERAL.—The term "customer" means—

(i) the person or entity that contracts with the home service provider for mobile telecommunications services; or

(ii) if the end user of mobile telecommunications services is not the contracting party, the end user of the mobile telecommunications service, but this clause applies only for the purpose of determining the place of primary use.

(B) The term "customer" does not include—

(i) a reseller of mobile telecommunications service; or

(ii) a serving carrier under an arrangement to serve the customer outside the home service provider's licensed service area.

(3) DESIGNATED DATABASE PROVIDER.—The term "designated database provider" means a corporation, association, or other entity representing all the political subdivisions of a State that is—

(A) responsible for providing an electronic database prescribed in section 119(a) if the State has not provided such electronic database; and

(B) approved by municipal and county associations or leagues of the State whose responsibility it would otherwise be to provide such database prescribed by sections 116 through 126 of this title.

(4) ENHANCED ZIP CODE.—The term "enhanced zip code" means a United States postal zip code of 9 or more digits.

(5) HOME SERVICE PROVIDER.—The term "home service provider" means the facilities-based carrier or reseller with which the customer contracts for the provision of mobile telecommunications services.

(6) LICENSED SERVICE AREA.—The term "licensed service area" means the geographic area in which the home service provider is authorized by law or contract to provide commercial mobile radio service to the customer.

(7) MOBILE TELECOMMUNICATIONS SERVICE.—The term "mobile telecommunications service" means commercial mobile radio service,

as defined in section 20.3 of title 47 of the Code of Federal Regulations as in effect on June 1, 1999.

(8) PLACE OF PRIMARY USE.—The term "place of primary use" means the street address representative of where the customer's use of the mobile telecommunications service primarily occurs, which must be—

(A) the residential street address or the primary business street address of the customer; and

(B) within the licensed service area of the home service provider.

(9) PREPAID TELEPHONE CALLING SERVICES.— The term "prepaid telephone calling service" means the right to purchase exclusively telecommunications services that must be paid for in advance, that enables the origination of calls using an access number, authorization code, or both, whether manually or electronically dialed, if the remaining amount of units of service that have been prepaid is known by the provider of the prepaid service on a continuous basis.

(10) RESELLER.—The term "reseller"—

(A) means a provider who purchases telecommunications services from another telecommunications service provider and then resells, uses as a component part of, or integrates the purchased services into a mobile telecommunications service; and

(B) does not include a serving carrier with which a home service provider arranges for the services to its customers outside the home service provider's licensed service area.

(11) SERVING CARRIER.—The term "serving carrier" means a facilities-based carrier providing mobile telecommunications service to a customer outside a home service provider's or reseller's licensed service area.

(12) TAXING JURISDICTION.—The term "taxing jurisdiction" means any of the several States, the District of Columbia, or any territory or possession of the United States, any municipality, city, county, township, parish, transportation district, or assessment jurisdiction, or any other political subdivision within the territorial limits of the United States with the authority to impose a tax, charge, or fee.

(Added Pub. L. 106–252, §2(a), July 28, 2000, 114 Stat. 631.)

EFFECTIVE DATE; APPLICATION OF AMENDMENT

Section effective July 28, 2000, and applicable only to customer bills issued after the first day of the first month beginning more than 2 years after July 28, 2000, see section 3 of Pub. L. 106–252, set out as a note under section 116 of this title.

§ 125. Nonseverability

If a court of competent jurisdiction enters a final judgment on the merits that—

(1) is based on Federal law;

(2) is no longer subject to appeal; and

(3) substantially limits or impairs the essential elements of sections 116 through 126 of this title,

then sections 116 through 126 of this title are invalid and have no legal effect as of the date of entry of such judgment.

(Added Pub. L. 106–252, §2(a), July 28, 2000, 114 Stat. 632.)

EFFECTIVE DATE; APPLICATION OF AMENDMENT

Section effective July 28, 2000, and applicable only to customer bills issued after the first day of the first month beginning more than 2 years after July 28, 2000, see section 116 of this title. Pub. L. 106–252, set out as a note under section 116 of this title.

§ 126. No inference

(a) INTERNET TAX FREEDOM ACT.—Nothing in sections 116 through this section of this title shall be construed as bearing on Congressional intent in enacting the Internet Tax Freedom Act or to modify or supersede the operation of such Act.

(b) TELECOMMUNICATIONS ACT OF 1996.—Nothing in sections 116 through this section of this title shall limit or otherwise affect the implementation of the Telecommunications Act of 1996 or the amendments made by such Act.

(Added Pub. L. 106–252, §2(a), July 28, 2000, 114 Stat. 632.)

REFERENCES IN TEXT

The Internet Tax Freedom Act, referred to in subsec. (a), is title XI of Pub. L. 105–277, div. C, Oct. 21, 1998, 112 Stat. 2681–719, which is set out as a note under section 151 of Title 47, Telegraphs, Telephones, and Radiotelegraphs.

The Telecommunications Act of 1996, referred to in subsec. (b), is Pub. L. 104–104, Feb. 8, 1996, 110 Stat. 56. For complete classification of this Act to the Code, see Short Title of 1996 Amendment note set out under section 609 of Title 47, Telegraphs, Telephones, and Radiotelegraphs, and Tables.

EFFECTIVE DATE; APPLICATION OF AMENDMENT

Section effective July 28, 2000, and applicable only to customer bills issued after the first day of the first month beginning more than 2 years after July 28, 2000, see section 3 of Pub. L. 106–252, set out as a note under section 116 of this title.

CHAPTER 5—OFFICIAL TERRITORIAL PAPERS

AMENDMENTS

1951—Chapter added by act Oct. 31, 1951, ch. 655, §12, 65 Stat. 713.

SIMILAR PROVISIONS; REPEAL; SAVING CLAUSE; DELEGATION OF FUNCTIONS; TRANSFER OF PROPERTY AND PERSONNEL

Similar provisions were contained in former chapter 5, comprising former sections 141 to 146, which was set out here but which was not a part of this title. Former sections 141 to 146 were derived from: acts Mar. 3, 1925, ch. 419, §§1, 2, 43 Stat. 1104; Mar. 3, 1925, ch. 419, §§3, 4, as added Feb. 28, 1929, ch. 385, 45 Stat. 1412, 1413; Feb. 28, 1929, ch. 385, 45 Stat. 1412 (in addition to the provisions added to said act Mar. 3, 1925); Mar. 22, 1935, ch. 39, §1 (part), 49 Stat. 69; Feb. 14, 1936, ch. 70, 49 Stat. 1139; May 15, 1936, ch. 405, §1 (part), 49 Stat. 1311; June 16, 1937, ch. 359, §1 (part), 50 Stat. 262, 263; June 28, 1937, ch. 386, 50 Stat. 323, 324; Apr. 27, 1938, ch. 180, §1 (part), 52 Stat.

249; June 29, 1939, ch. 248, title I (part), 53 Stat. 886; July
31, 1945, ch. 336, 59 Stat. 510, 511; 1946 Proc. No. 2714, Dec.
31, 1946, 12 F.R. 1; act Oct. 28, 1949, ch. 782, title XI,
§ 1106(a), 63 Stat. 972; 1950 Reorg. Plan No. 20, § 1, eff.
May 24, 1950, 15 F.R. 3178, 64 Stat. 1272; act July 7, 1950,
ch. 452, 64 Stat. 320. All of the foregoing provisions,
with the exception of 1946 Proc. No. 2714, act Oct. 28,
1949, § 1106(a), and 1950 Reorg. Plan No. 20, § 1, were repealed by act Oct. 31, 1951, ch. 655, § 56(k)(1)–(11), 65 Stat.
730. Subsec. (l) of section 56 provided that the repeal
should not affect any rights or liabilities existing under
the repealed statutes on the effective date of the repeal
(Oct. 31, 1951). For delegation of functions under the repealed statutes, and for transfer of records, property,
personnel, and funds, see sections 3 and 4 of said 1950
Reorg. Plan No. 20, set out in the Appendix to Title 5,
Government Organization and Employees.

§ 141. Collection, preparation and publication

The Archivist of the United States, hereinafter referred to in this chapter as the "Archivist", shall continue to completion the work of
collecting, editing, copying, and suitably ar-
ranging for issuance as a Government publication, the official papers relating to the Territories from which States of the United States
were formed, in the national archives, as listed
in Parker's "Calendar of Papers in Washington"
Archives Relating to the Territories of the
United States (to 1873)", being publication num-
bered 148 of the Carnegie Institution of Washington, together with such additional papers of like
character which may be found.

(Added Oct. 31, 1951, ch. 655, § 12, 65 Stat. 713;
amended Pub. L. 98–497, title I, § 107(f), Oct. 19,
1984, 98 Stat. 2292.)

AMENDMENTS

1984—Pub. L. 98–497 substituted "Archivist of the
United States" and "Archivist" for "Administrator of
General Services" and "Administrator", respectively.

EFFECTIVE DATE OF 1984 AMENDMENT

Amendment by Pub. L. 98–497 effective Apr. 1, 1985,
see section 301 of Pub. L. 98–497, set out as a note under
section 2102 of Title 44, Public Printing and Documents.

SIMILAR PROVISIONS; REPEAL; SAVING CLAUSE; DELEGA-
TION OF FUNCTIONS; TRANSFER OF PROPERTY AND PER-
SONNEL

See note preceding this section.

§ 142. Appointment of experts

For the purpose of carrying on the work prescribed by section 141 of this title, the Archivist,
without regard to the Classification Act of 1949
and the civil service laws and regulations there-
under, may engage the services, either in or outside of the District of Columbia, of not to exceed
five historical experts who are especially in-
formed on the various phases of the territorial
history of the United States and are especially
qualified for the editorial work necessary in ar-
ranging such territorial papers for publication.

(Added Oct. 31, 1951, ch. 655, § 12, 65 Stat. 714;
amended Pub. L. 98–497, title I, § 107(f), Oct. 19,
1984, 98 Stat. 2292.)

REFERENCES IN TEXT

The Classification Act of 1949, referred to in text, is
act Oct. 28, 1949, ch. 782, 63 Stat. 954, which was repealed
by Pub. L. 89–554, § 8(a), Sept. 6, 1966, 80 Stat. 632, and
reenacted by the first section thereof as chapter 51 and

subchapter III of chapter 53 of Title 5, Government Organization and Employees.

AMENDMENTS

1984—Pub. L. 98–497 substituted "Archivist" for "Administrator".

EFFECTIVE DATE OF 1984 AMENDMENT

Amendment by Pub. L. 98–497 effective Apr. 1, 1985,
see section 301 of Pub. L. 98–497, set out as a note under
section 2102 of Title 44, Public Printing and Documents.

SIMILAR PROVISIONS; REPEAL; SAVING CLAUSE; DELEGA-
TION OF FUNCTIONS; TRANSFER OF PROPERTY AND PER-
SONNEL

See note preceding section 141 of this title.

§ 143. Employment and utilization of other per-
sonnel; cost of copy reading and indexing

(a) In carrying out his functions under this
chapter, the Archivist may employ such clerical
assistants as may be necessary.
(b) The work of copy reading and index making for the publication of the papers described in
section 141 of this title shall be done by the regular editorial staff of the National Archives and
Records Administration, and the cost of this
particular phase of the work (prorated each
month according to the number of hours spent
and the annual salaries of the clerks employed)
shall be charged against the annual appropria-
tions made under section 146 of this title.

(Added Oct. 31, 1951, ch. 655, § 12, 65 Stat. 714;
amended Pub. L. 98–497, title I, § 107(f), Oct. 19,
1984, 98 Stat. 2292.)

AMENDMENTS

1984—Subsec. (a). Pub. L. 98–497 substituted "Archivist" for "Administrator".
Subsec. (b). Pub. L. 98–497 substituted "National Archives and Records Administration" for "General Services Administration".

EFFECTIVE DATE OF 1984 AMENDMENT

Amendment by Pub. L. 98–497 effective Apr. 1, 1985,
see section 301 of Pub. L. 98–497, set out as a note under
section 2102 of Title 44, Public Printing and Documents.

SIMILAR PROVISIONS; REPEAL; SAVING CLAUSE; DELEGA-
TION OF FUNCTIONS; TRANSFER OF PROPERTY AND PER-
SONNEL

See note preceding section 141 of this title.

§ 144. Cooperation of departments and agencies

The heads of the several executive departments and independent agencies and establishments shall cooperate with the Archivist in the
work prescribed by section 141 of this title by
permitting access to any records deemed by him
to be necessary to the completion of such work.

(Added Oct. 31, 1951, ch. 655, § 12, 65 Stat. 714;
amended Pub. L. 98–497, title I, § 107(f), Oct. 19,
1984, 98 Stat. 2292.)

AMENDMENTS

1984—Pub. L. 98–497 substituted "Archivist" for "Administrator".

EFFECTIVE DATE OF 1984 AMENDMENT

Amendment by Pub. L. 98–497 effective Apr. 1, 1985,
see section 301 of Pub. L. 98–497, set out as a note under
section 2102 of Title 44, Public Printing and Documents.

§ 145. Printing and distribution

(a) The Public Printer shall print and bind each volume of the official papers relating to the Territories of the United States as provided for in this chapter, of which—

(1) four hundred and twenty copies shall be delivered to the Superintendent of Documents, Government Printing Office, for distribution, on the basis of one copy each, and as directed by the Archivist, to those historical associations, commissions, museums, or libraries and other nondepository libraries, not to exceed eight in number within each State, Territory, or Possession, which have been or may be designated by the Governor thereof to receive such copies;

(2) one hundred copies shall be delivered to the National Archives and Records Administration for the use of that Administration; and

(3) one hundred copies shall be delivered to the Superintendent of Documents for distribution in such manner and number as may be authorized and directed by the Joint Committee on Printing.

(b) The historical associations, commissions, museums, or libraries and other nondepository libraries within each State, Territory, or Possession which have been or may be designated by the Governor thereof to receive the publications referred to in subsection (a) of this section, shall, during their existence, receive the succeeding volumes, the distribution of which shall be made by the Superintendent of Documents in accordance with lists of designations transmitted to him by the Archivist. A new designation may be made to the Archivist by the Governor only when a designated association, commission, museum, or library shall cease to exist, or when authorized by law.

(Added Oct. 31, 1951, ch. 655, § 12, 65 Stat. 714; amended Pub. L. 98–497, title I, § 107(f), Oct. 19, 1984, 98 Stat. 2292.)

AMENDMENTS

1984—Subsec. (a)(1). Pub. L. 98–497 substituted "Archivist" for "Administrator".
Subsec. (a)(2). Pub. L. 98–497 substituted "National Archives and Records Administration" for "General Services Administration".
Subsec. (b). Pub. L. 98–497 substituted "Archivist" for "Administrator" in two places.

EFFECTIVE DATE OF 1984 AMENDMENT

Amendment by Pub. L. 98–497 effective Apr. 1, 1985, see section 301 of Pub. L. 98–497, set out as a note under section 2102 of Title 44, Public Printing and Documents.

§ 146. Authorization of appropriations

For the purposes of this chapter, there are authorized to be appropriated, out of any money in the Treasury not otherwise appropriated, sums of not more than $50,000 for any one fiscal year.

(Added Oct. 31, 1951, ch. 655, § 12, 65 Stat. 715.)

Made in the USA
Las Vegas, NV
19 September 2023

77788938R00015